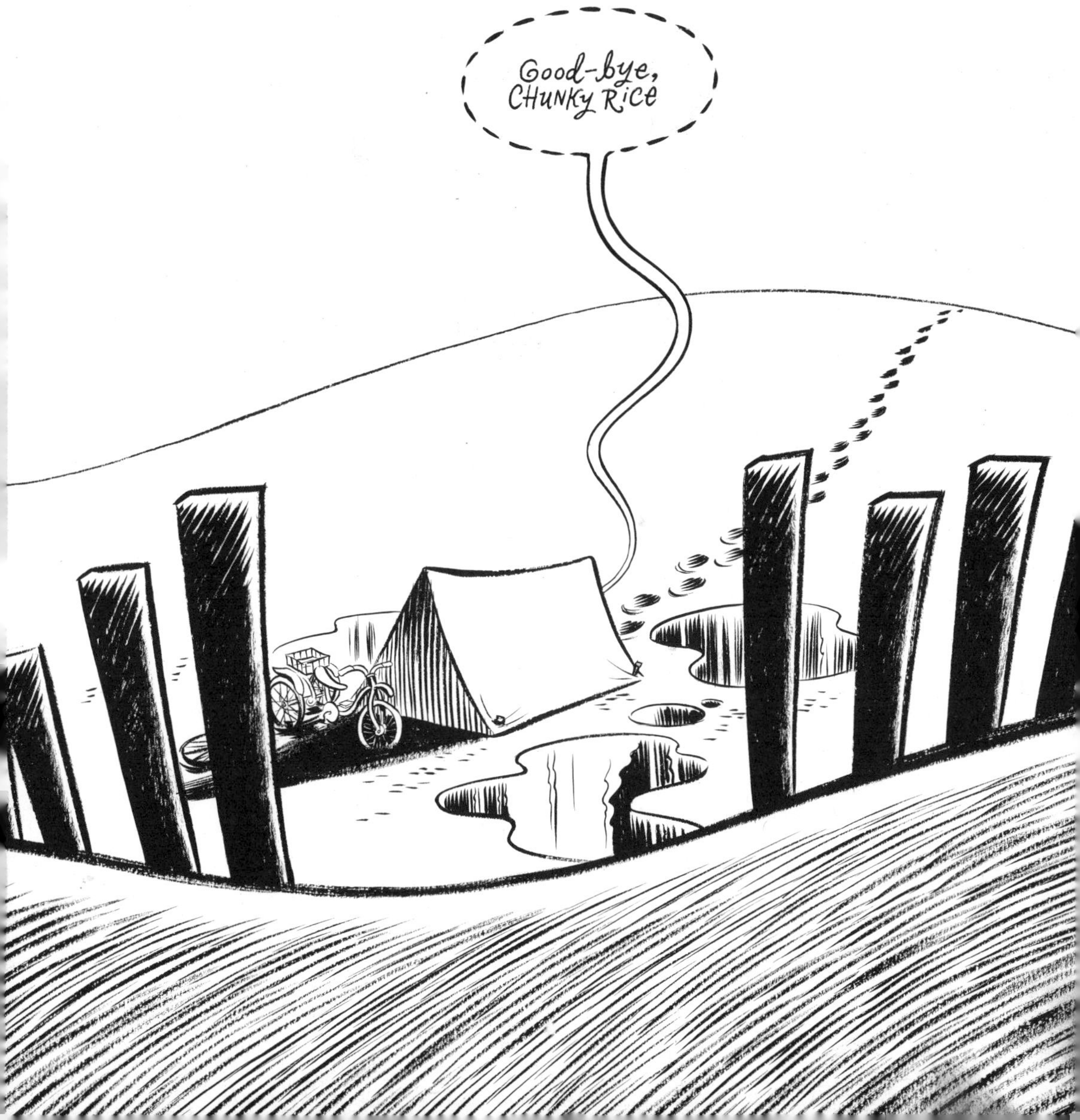
Good-bye,
CHUNKY RICE

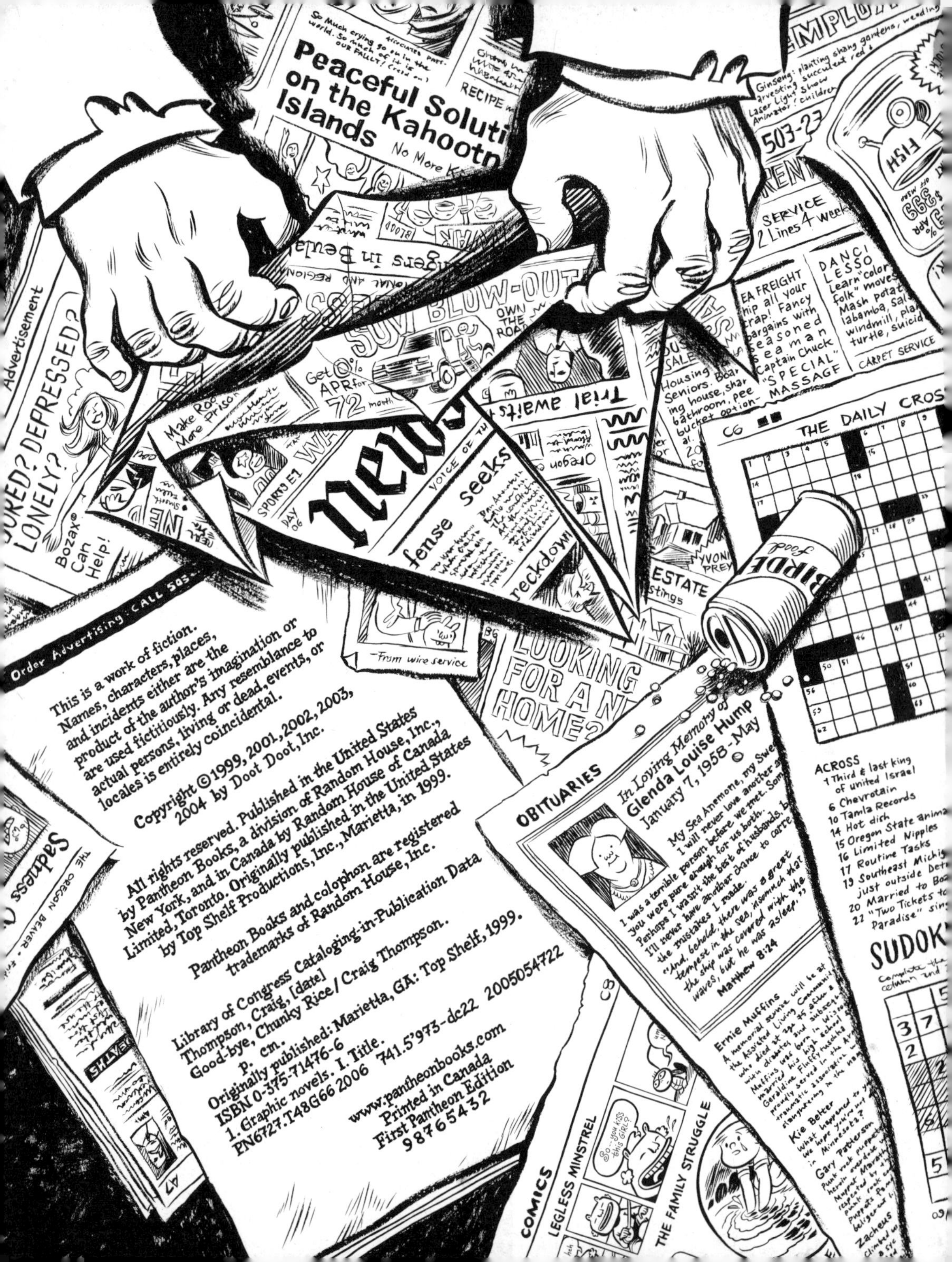
Peaceful Soluti
on the Kahootn
Islands
No More K
EMPLOY
503-27
RENT
SERVICE
2 Lines 4 Week
SUV BLOW-OUT
Get 0% APR for 72 month
Trial awaits
news
Advertisement
DEPRESSED?
LONELY?
Bozax® Can Help!
Order Advertising CALL 503
EA FREIGHT
hip all your crap! Fancy bargains with seasoned seaman Captain Chuck "SPECIAL" MASSAGE
CARPET SERVICE
THE DAILY CROS
ESTATE
LOOKING FOR A N HOME?
-From wire service
BIRDE Food
OBITUARIES
In Loving Memory of
Glenda Louise Hump
January 7, 1958 – May
ACROSS
1 Third & last king of united Israel
6 Chevrotain
10 Tamla Records
14 Hot dish
15 Oregon State anima
16 Limited Nipples
17 Routine Tasks
17 Southeast Michig
19 just outside Det
20 Married to Boz
22 "Two Tickets to Paradise" sing
SUDOK
THE OREGON BEAVER
COMICS
LEGLESS MINSTREL
THE FAMILY STRUGGLE

This is a work of fiction. Names, characters, places, and incidents either are the product of the author's imagination or are used fictitiously. Any resemblance to actual persons, living or dead, events, or locales is entirely coincidental.

 Published in the United States by Pantheon Books, a division of Random House, Inc., New York, and in Canada by Random House of Canada Limited, Toronto. Originally published in the United States by Top Shelf Productions, Inc., Marietta, in 1999.

Pantheon Books and colophon are registered trademarks of Random House, Inc.

Pantheon Books Cataloging-in-Publication Data

Library of Congress Cataloging-in-Publication Data
Thompson, Craig, [date]
Good-bye, Chunky Rice / Craig Thompson.
p. cm.
Originally published: Marietta, GA: Top Shelf, 1999.
ISBN 0-375-71476-6
1. Graphic novels. I. Title.
PN6727.T48G66 2006 741.5'973-dc22 2005054722

www.pantheonbooks.com
Printed in Canada
First Pantheon Edition
9 8 7 6 5 4 3 2

GOOD-BYE, CHUNKY, RICE

CRAIG THOMPSON

PANTHEON BOOKS, NEW YORK

This book is dedicated
to all of my friends
in Milwaukee, WI.

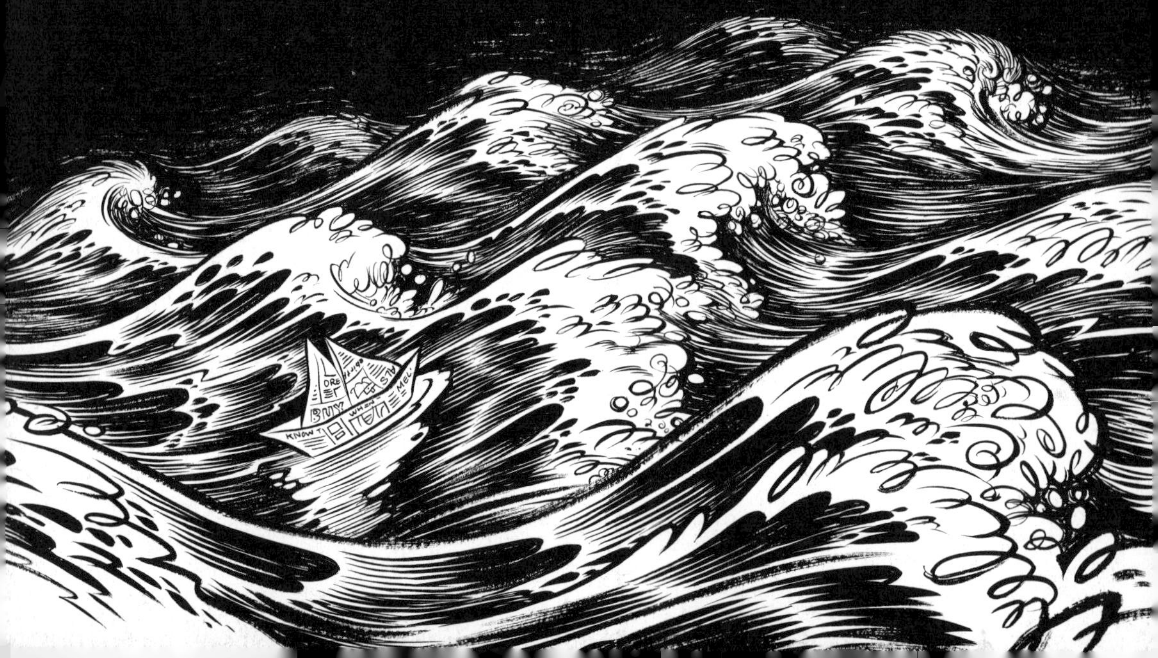

CLUNK

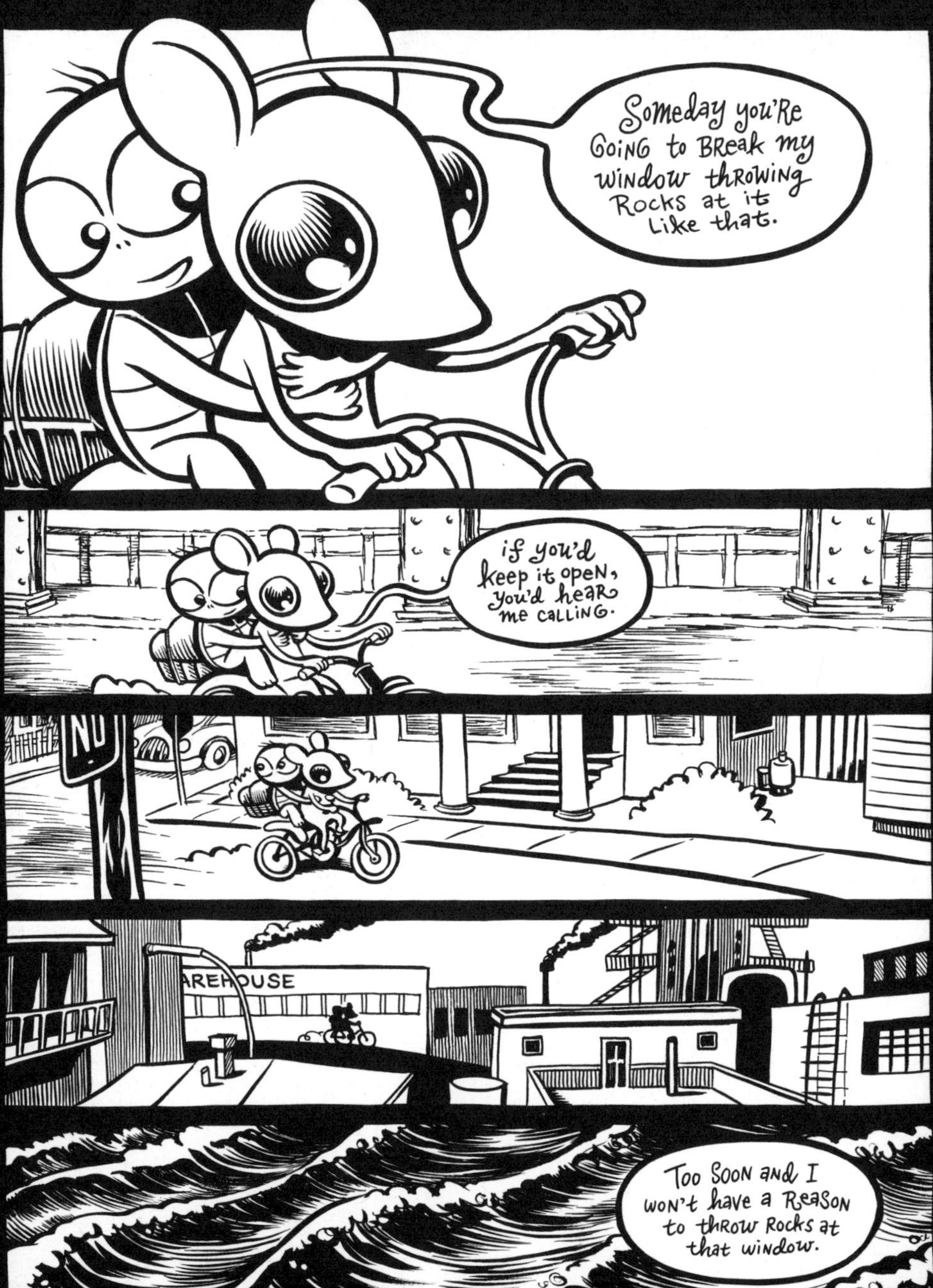
Someday you're going to break my window throwing rocks at it like that.
if you'd keep it open, you'd hear me calling.
AREHOUSE
Too soon and I won't have a reason to throw rocks at that window.

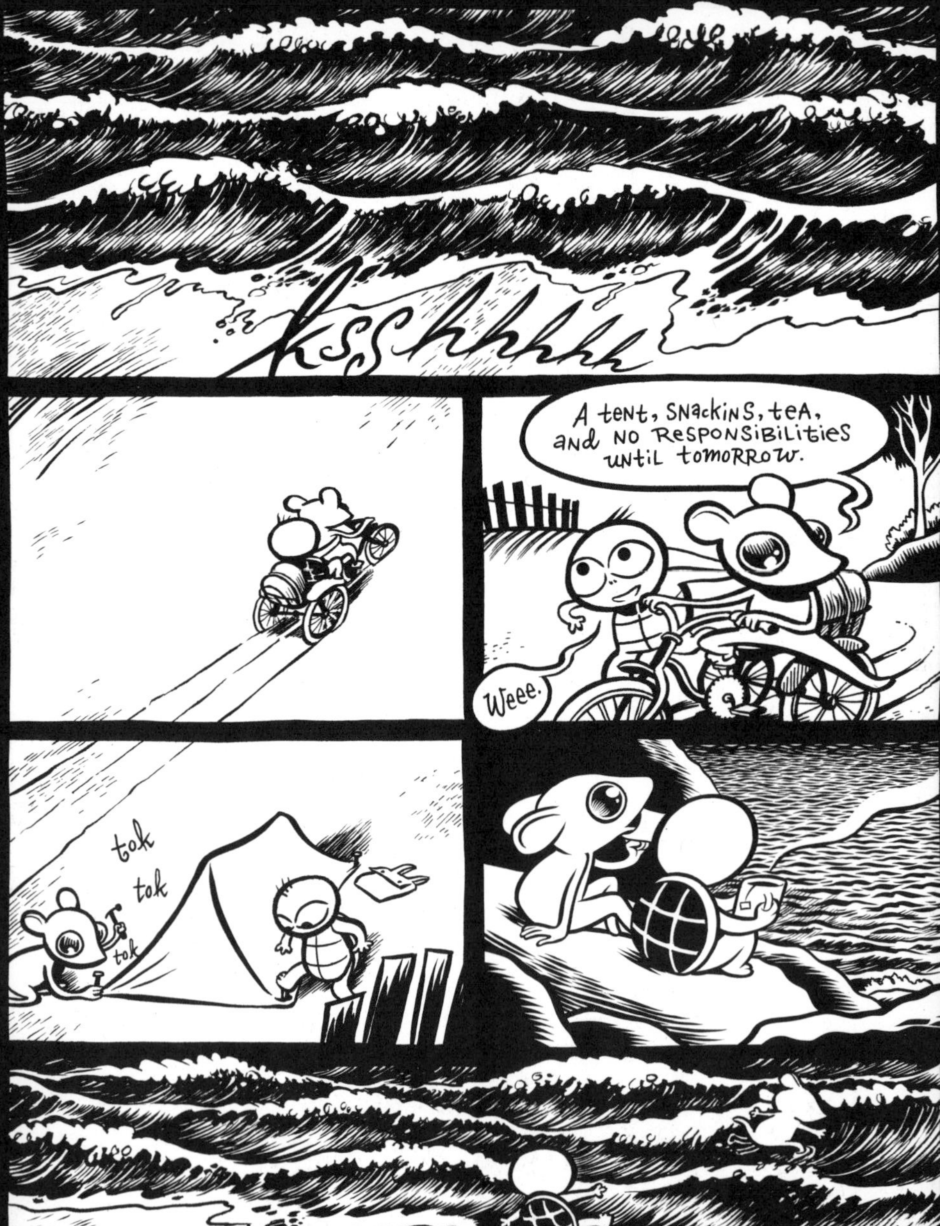
kSSchhhhh
A tent, SNackinS, tea, and NO ResponsiBilities until tomorrow.
Weee.
tok
tok
tok

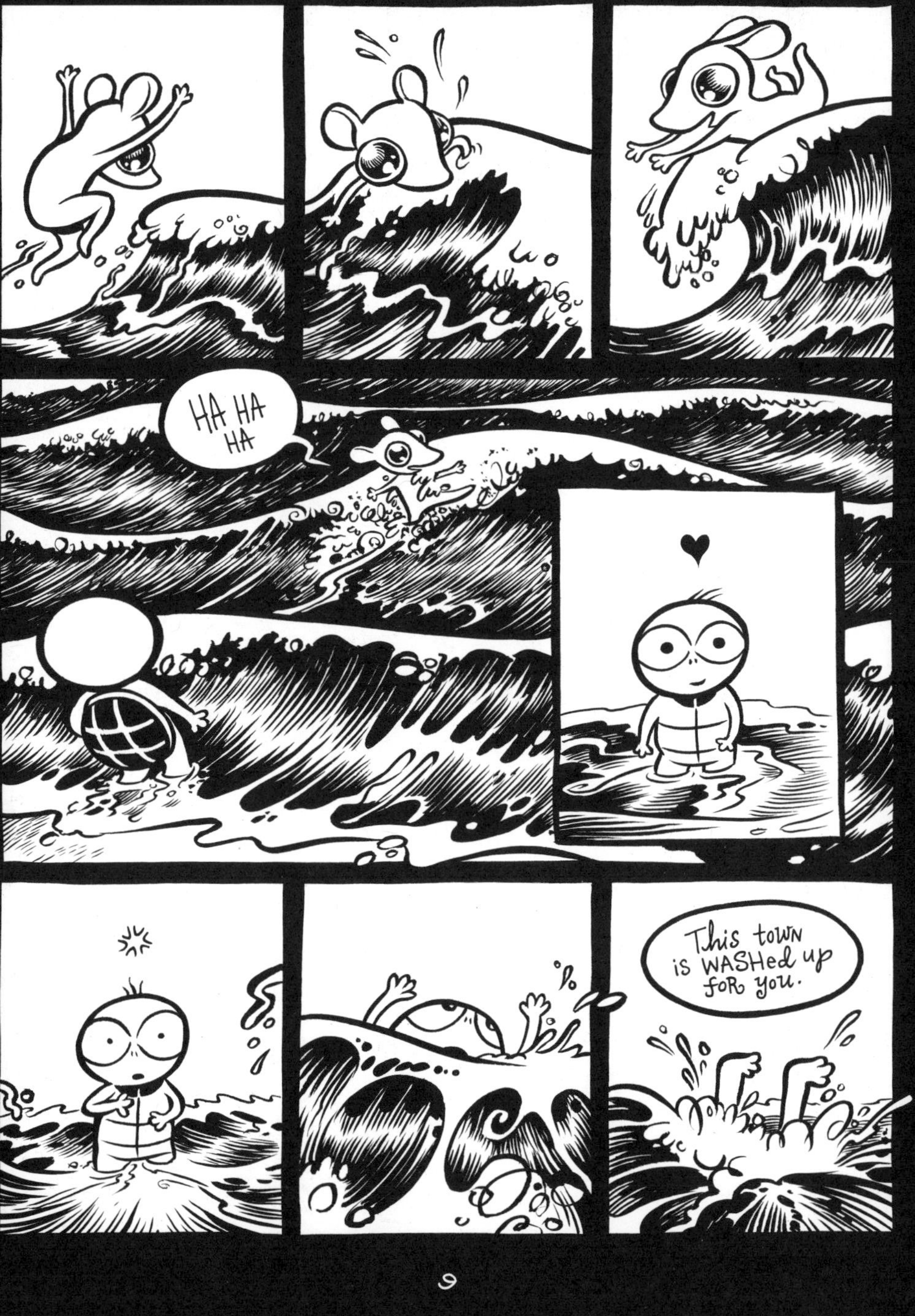
HA HA HA
This town is WASHed up for you.

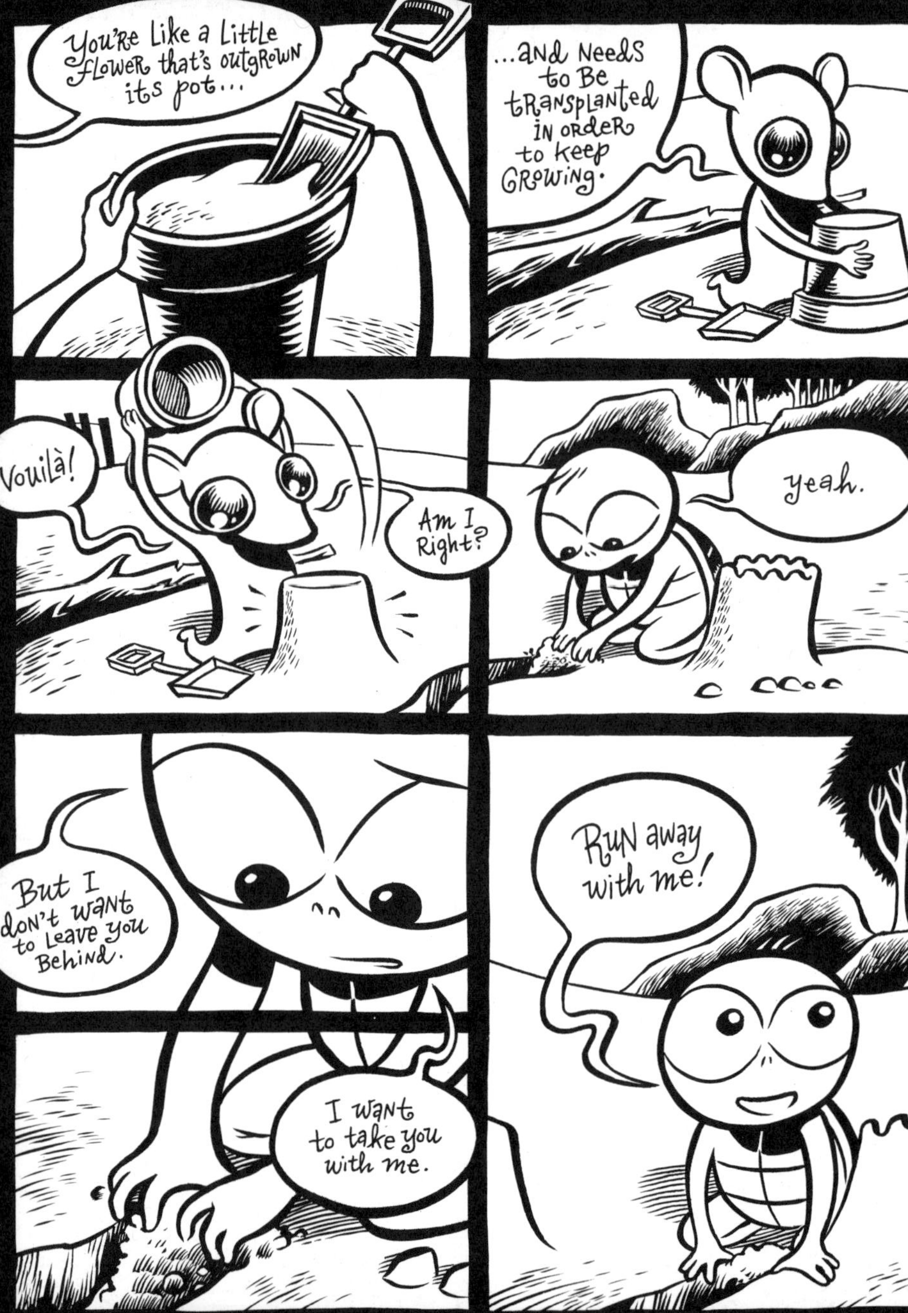
You're like a little flower that's outgrown its pot...
...and needs to be transplanted in order to keep growing.
Voilà!
Am I right?
yeah.
But I don't want to leave you behind.
I want to take you with me.
Run away with me!

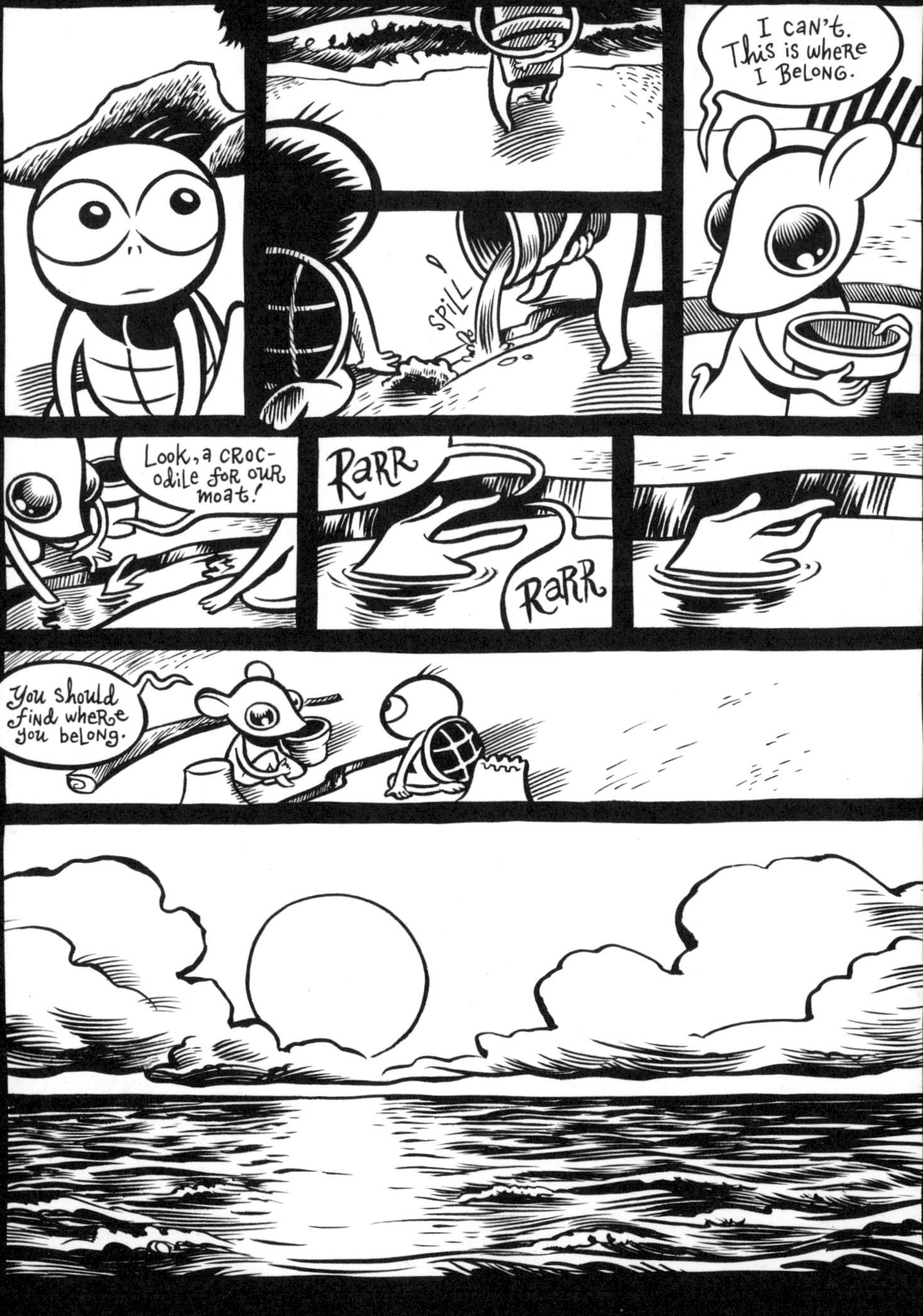
SPILL
I can't. This is where I belong.
Look, a croc-odile for our moat!
RARR
RARR
You should find where you belong.

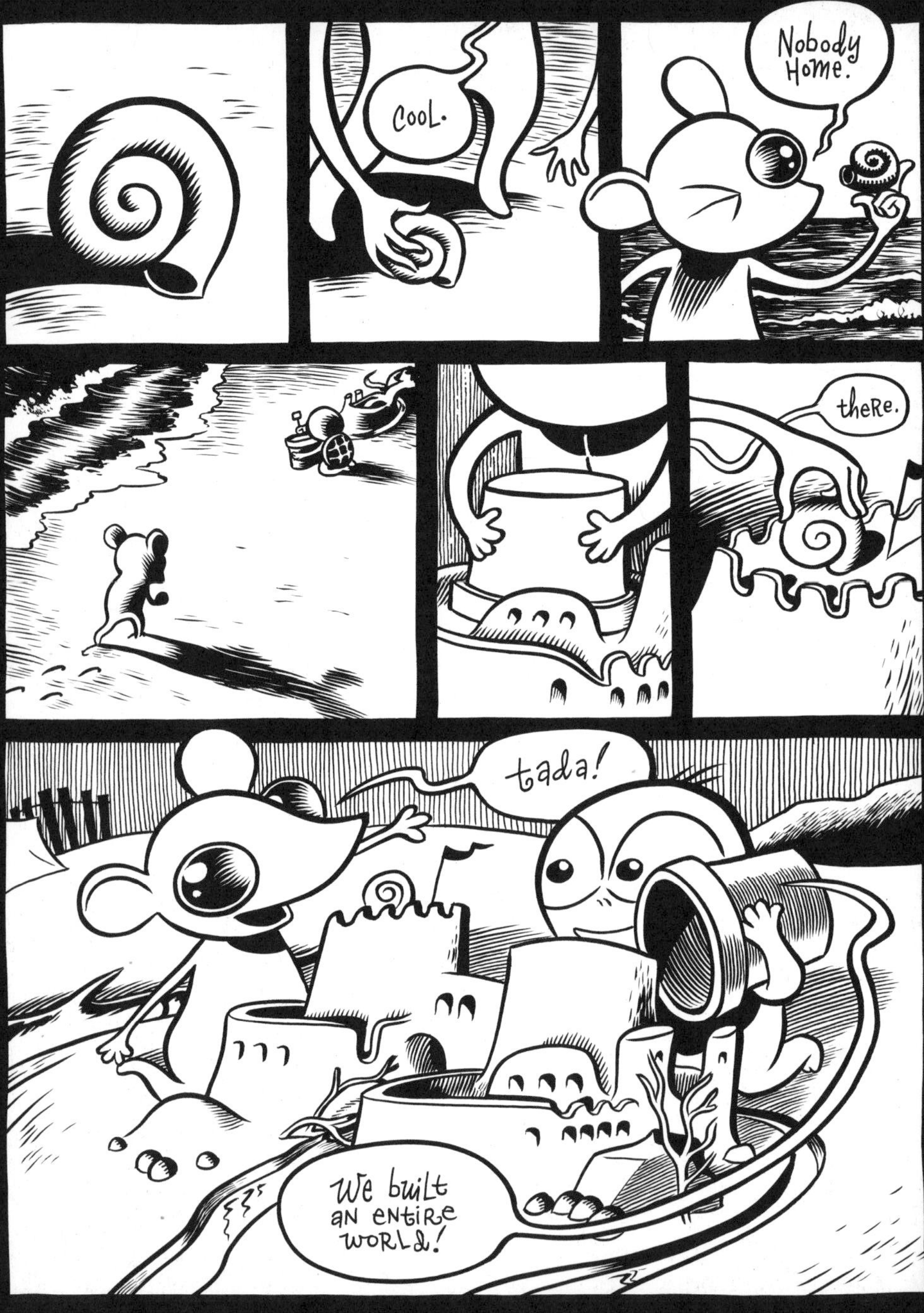

Cool.
Nobody Home.
there.
tada!
We built an entire world!

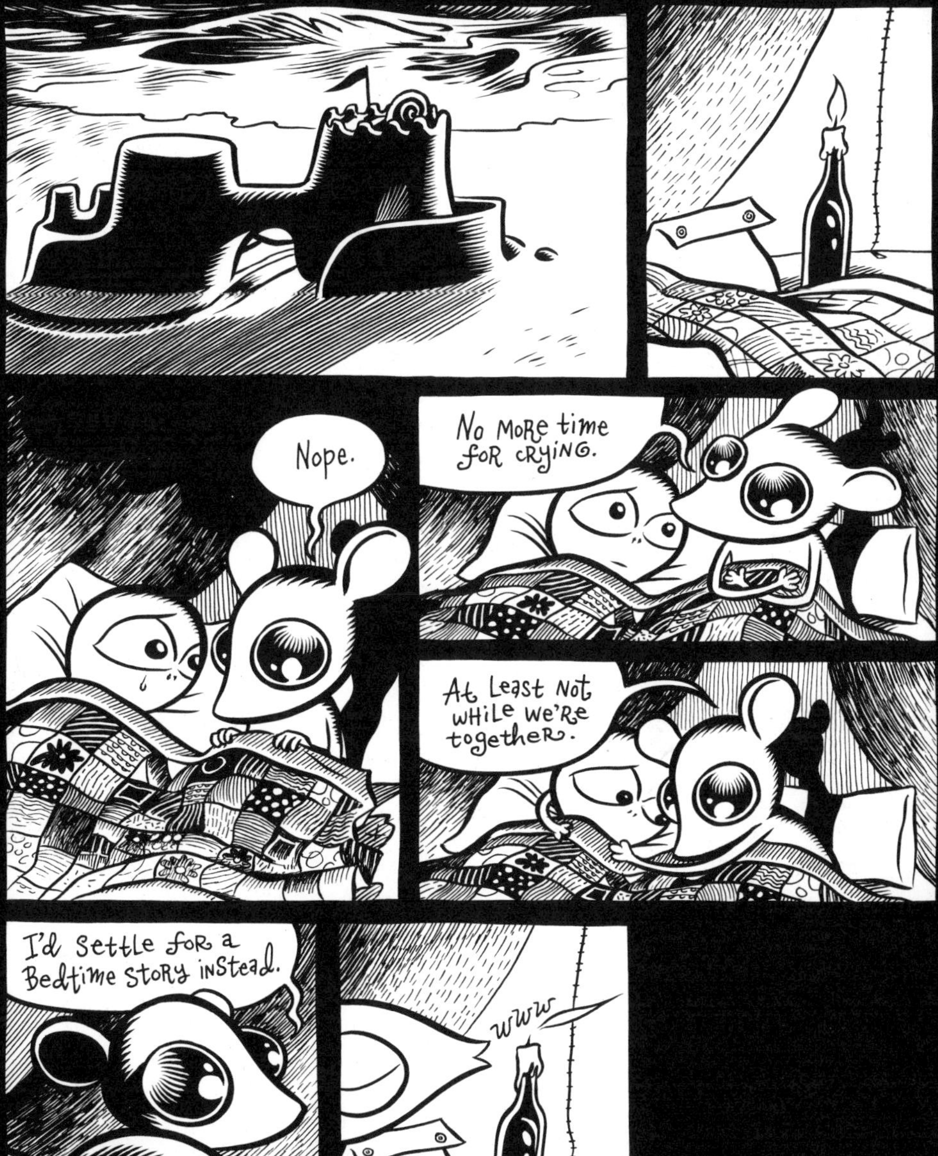

Nope.
No more time for crying.
At least not while we're together.
I'd settle for a bedtime story instead.
www

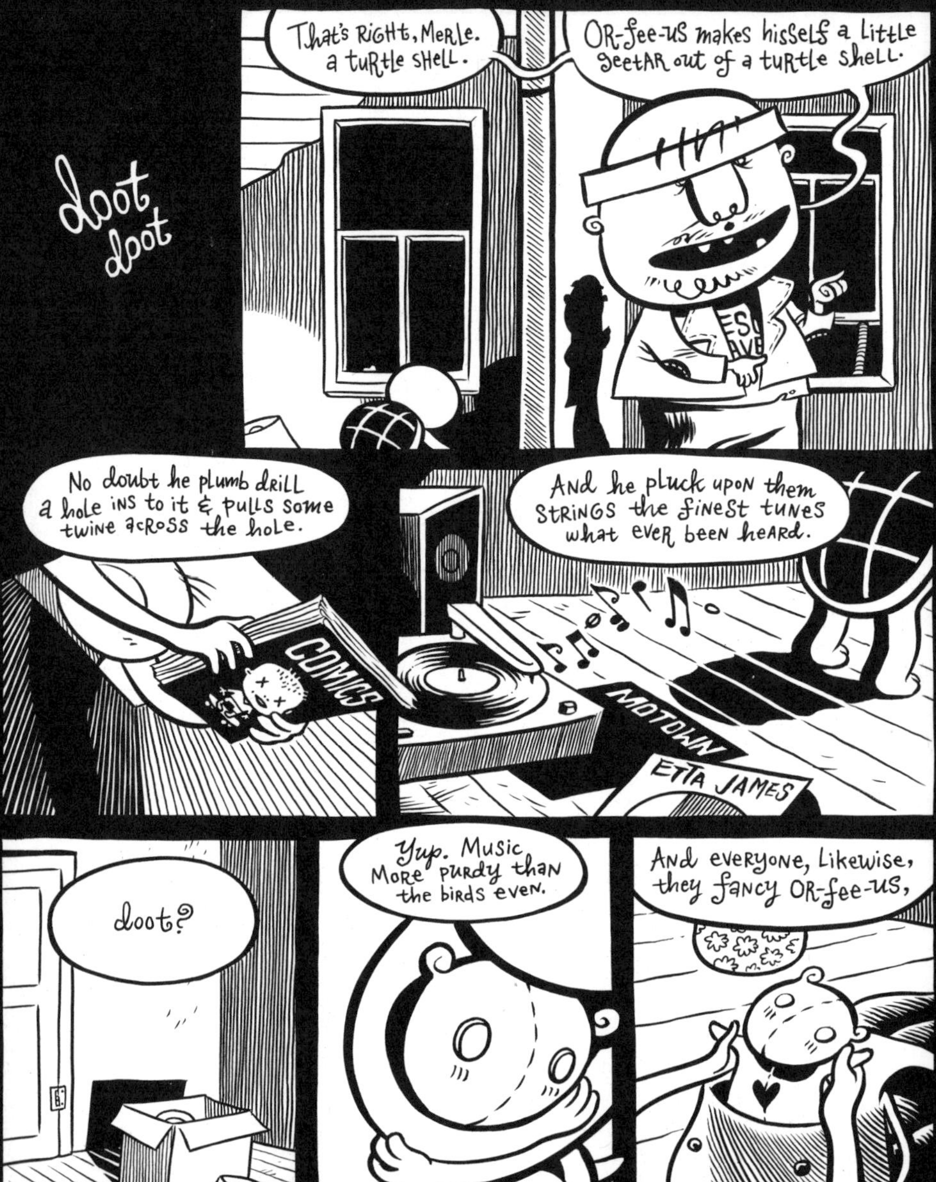
doot doot
That's RIGHT, MeRLe. a tuRtle sheLL.
OR-fee-us makes hisself a Little geetAR out of a tuRtle sheLL.
ESQ AVE
No doubt he plumb dRiLL a hole ins to it & puLLs some twine acRoss the hoLe.
And he pluck upon them stRings the finest tunes what eveR been heaRd.
COMICS
MOTOWN
ETTA JAMES
doot?
Yup. Music MoRe puRdy than the birds even.
And everyone, Likewise, they fancy OR-fee-us,

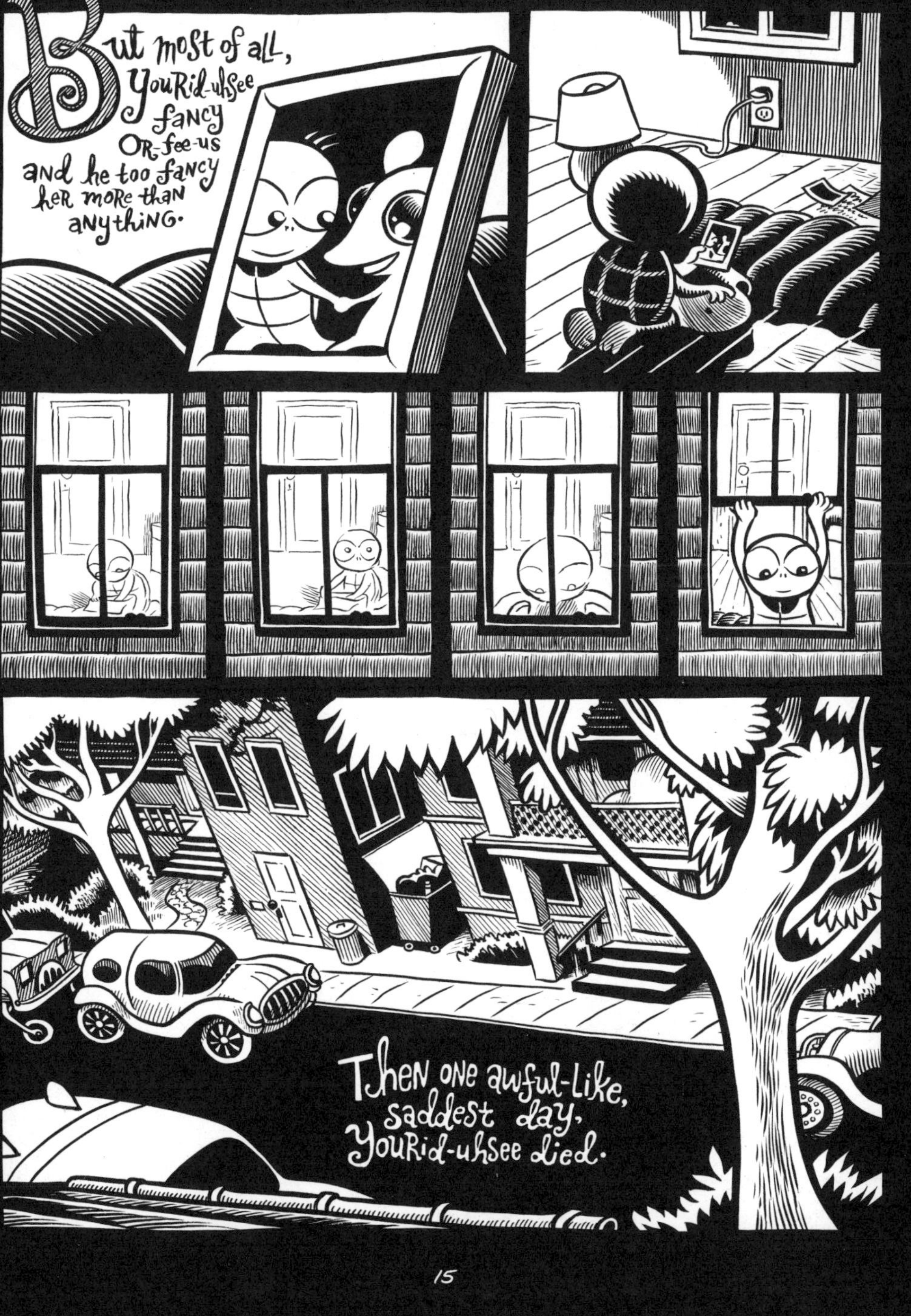
But most of all, YouRid-uhsee fancy OR-fee-us and he too fancy her more than anything.
Then one awful-like, saddest day, YouRid-uhsee died.

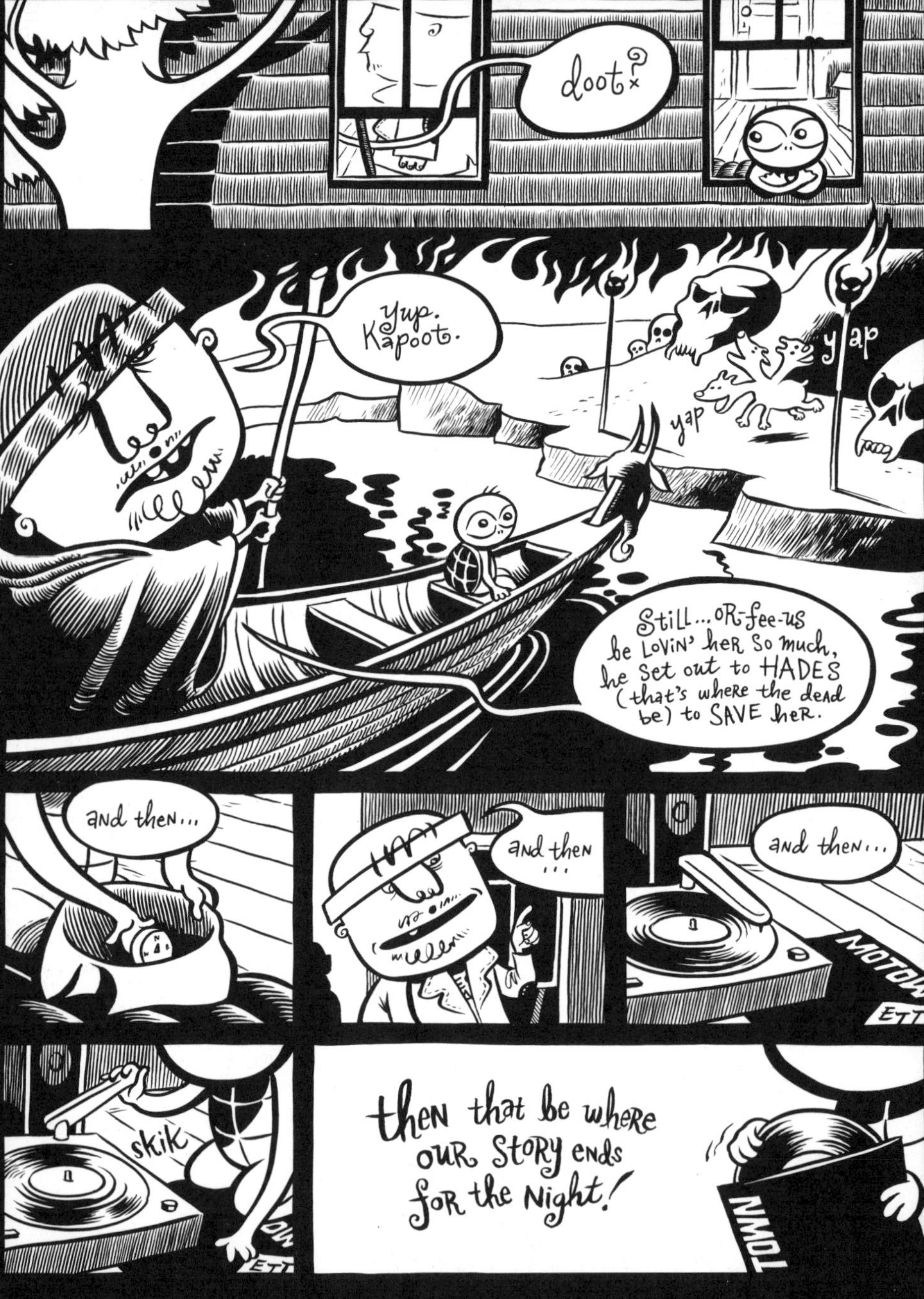
doot?
yup. Kapoot.
yap
yap
Still... OR-fee-us be LOVIN' her so much, he set out to HADES (that's where the dead be) to SAVE her.
and then...
and then ...
and then...
MOTOW
ETT
skik
then that be where OUR STORY ends for the Night!
TOWN

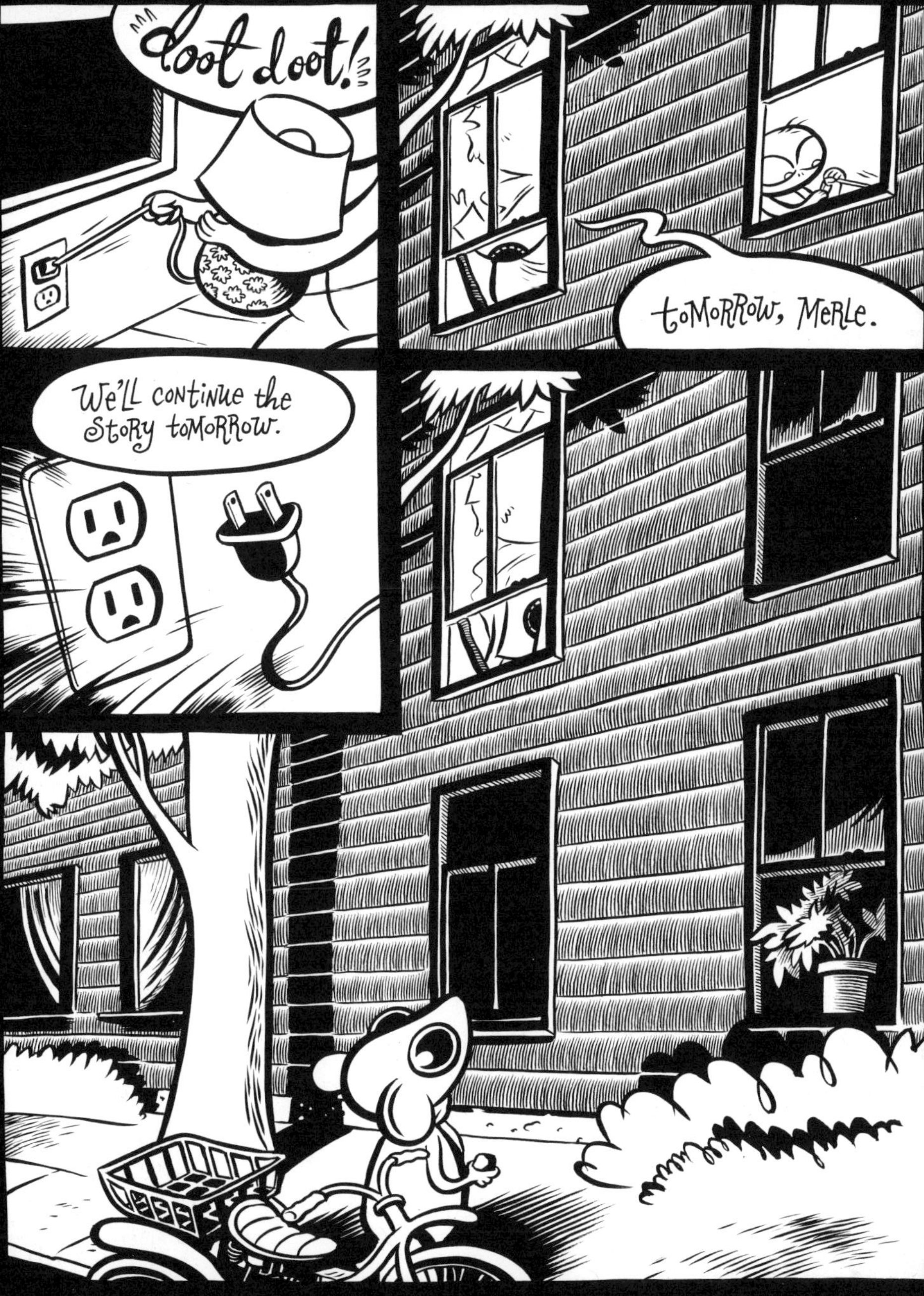
doot doot!
tomorrow, Merle.
We'll continue the story tomorrow.

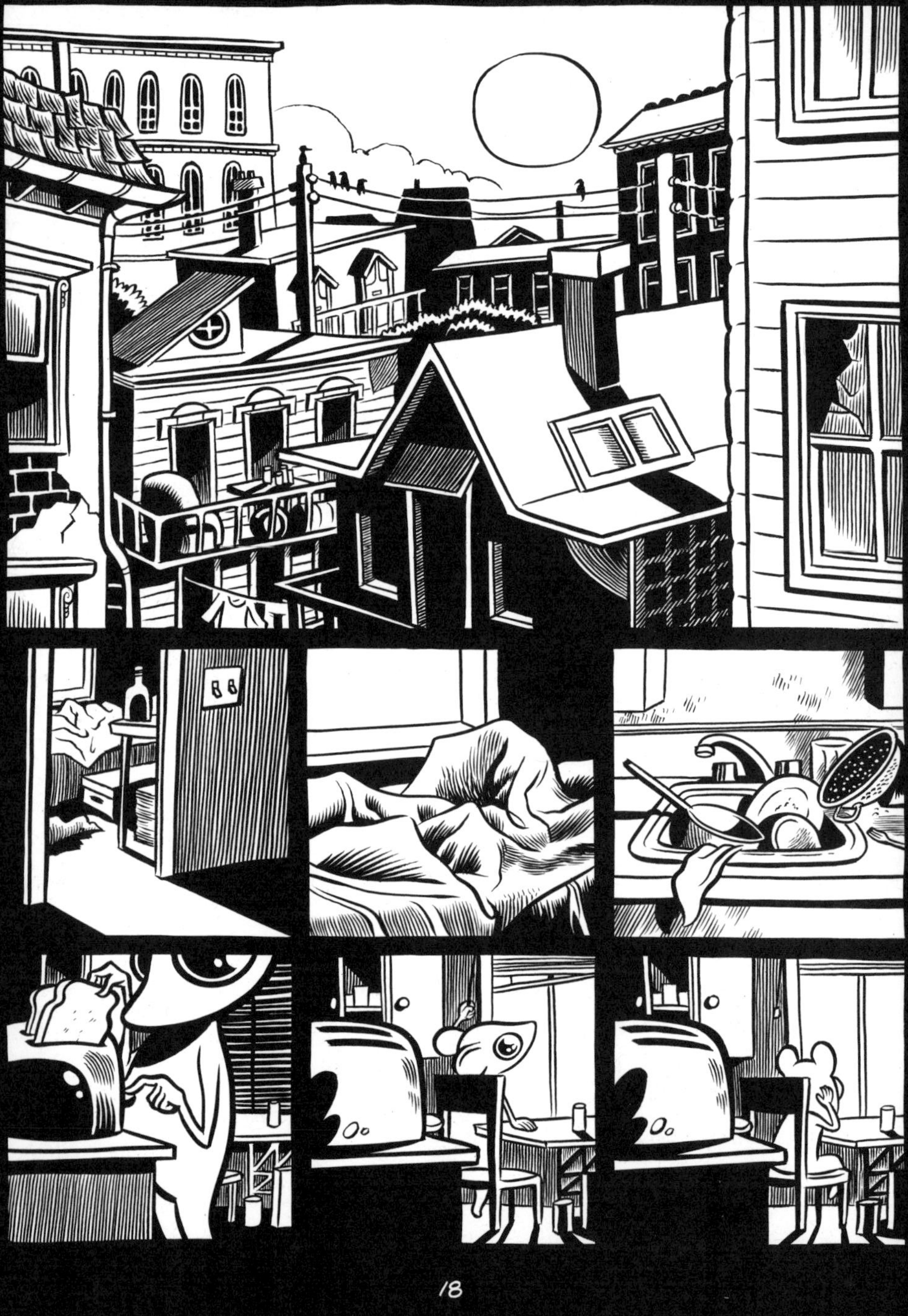

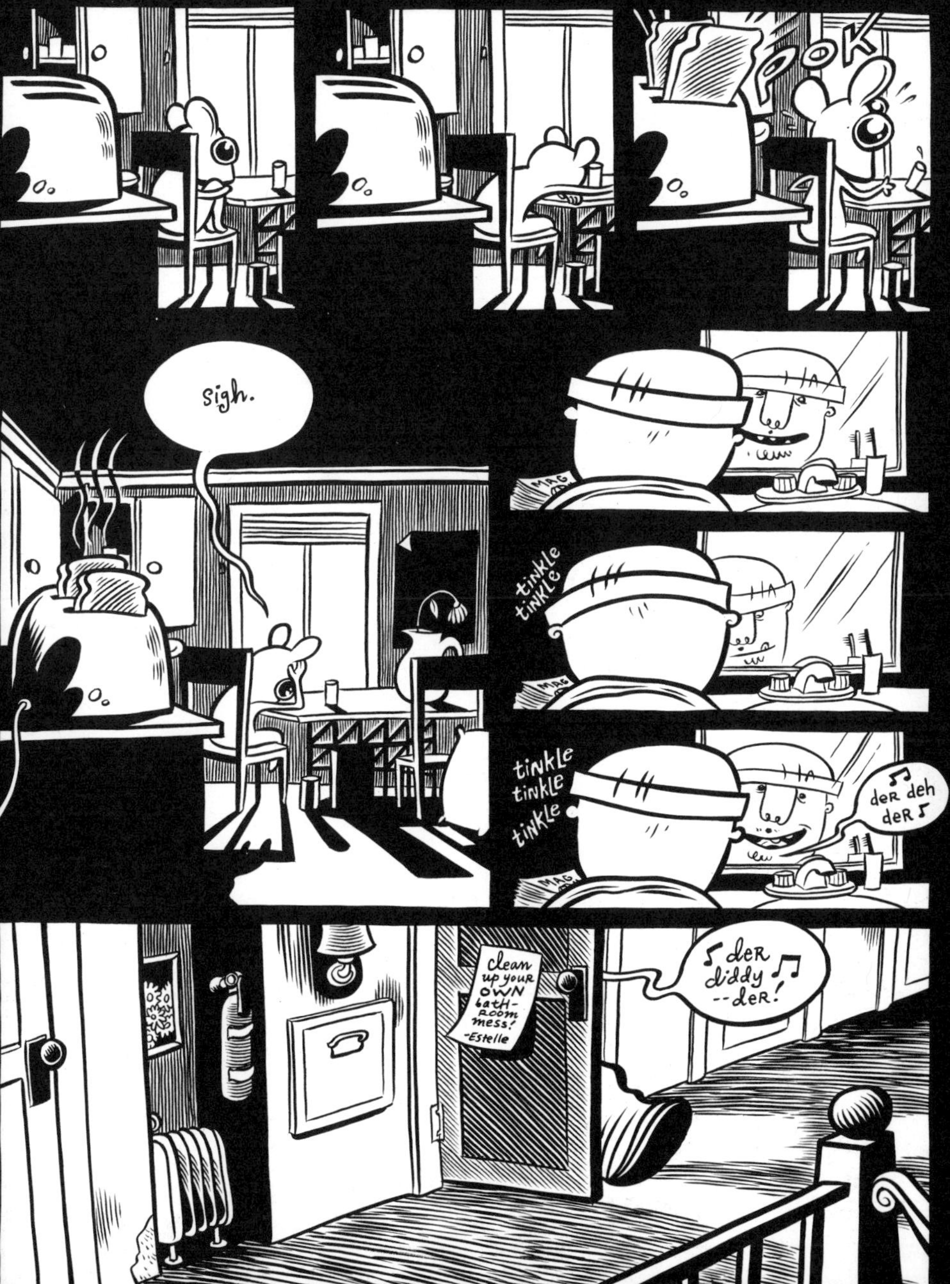
POK
sigh.
MAG
tinkle tinkle
tinkle tinkle tinkle
der deh der
clean up your OWN bath-room mess! -Estelle
der diddy --der!

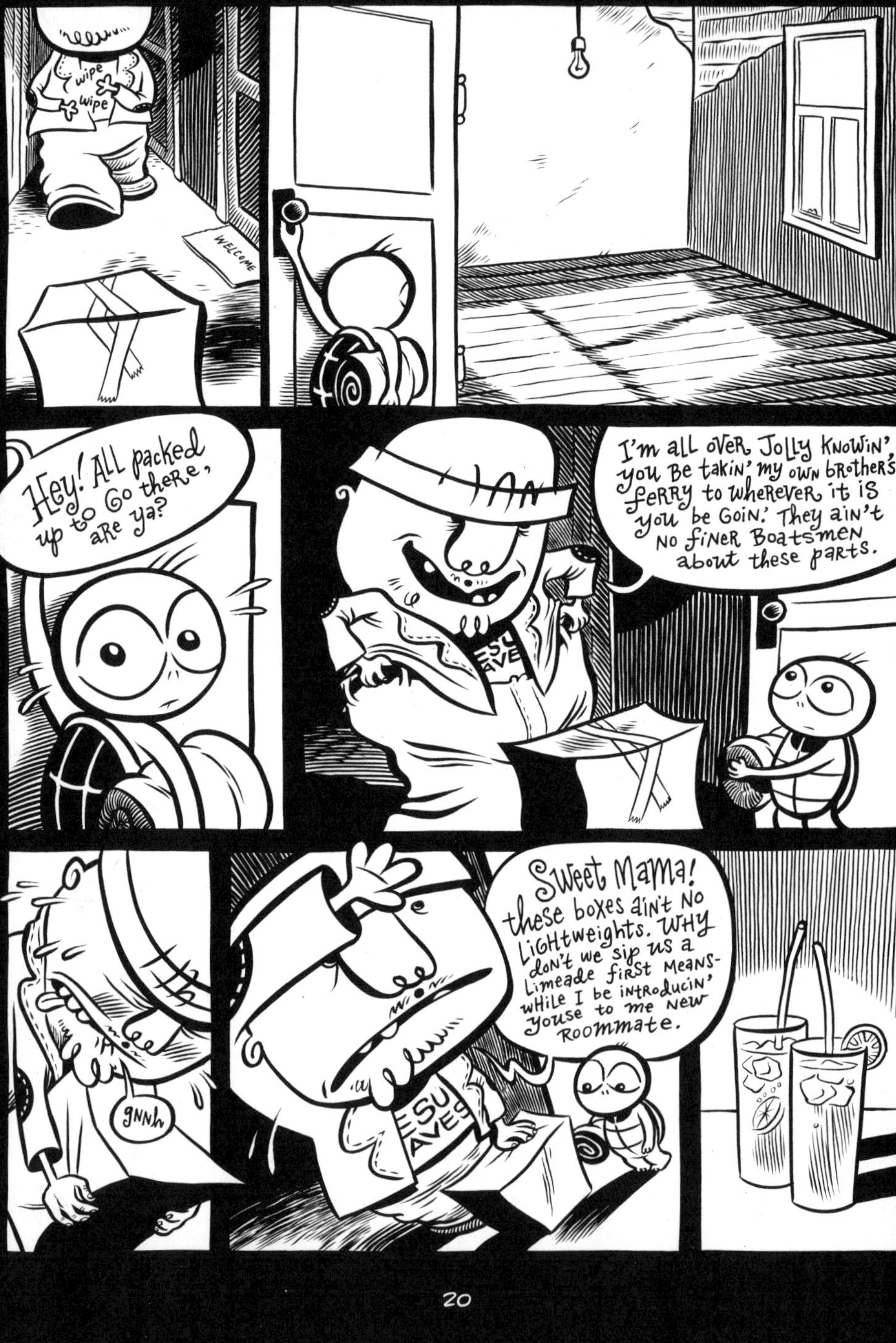
wipe
wipe
WELCOME
Hey! All packed up to Go there, are ya?
I'm all over Jolly knowin' you be takin' my own brother's ferry to wherever it is you be goin.' They ain't no finer Boatsmen about these parts.
gNNh
Sweet Mama! these boxes ain't no lightweights. Why don't we sip us a limeade first meanswhile I be introducin' youse to me new roommate.

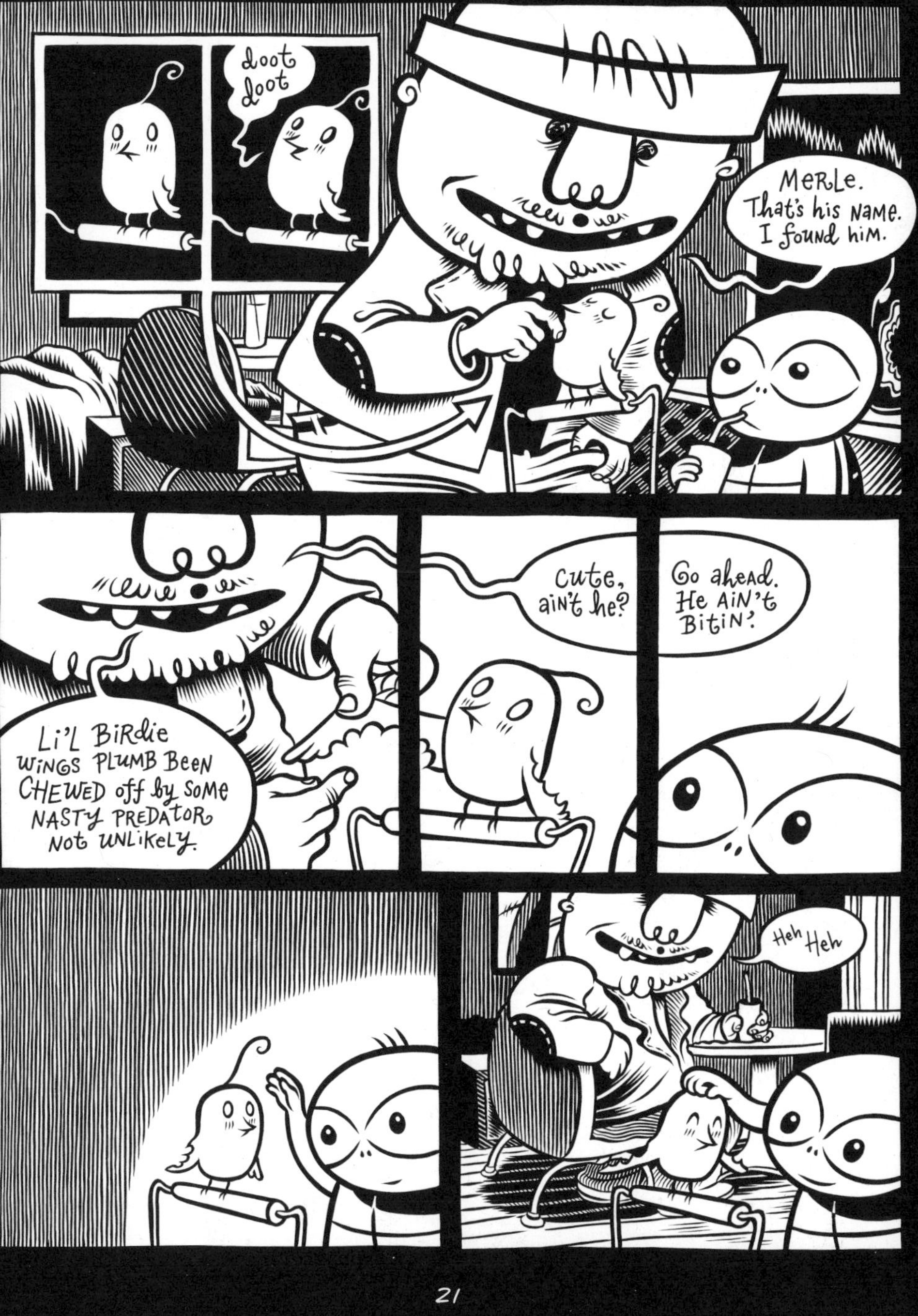
doot doot
MERLE. That's his NAME. I found him.
Li'L BIRdie WiNGS PLUMB BeeN CHEWED off by SOME NASTY PREDATOR NOT UNLiKeLY.
Cute, ain't he?
Go ahead. He AIN't BitiN'.
Heh Heh

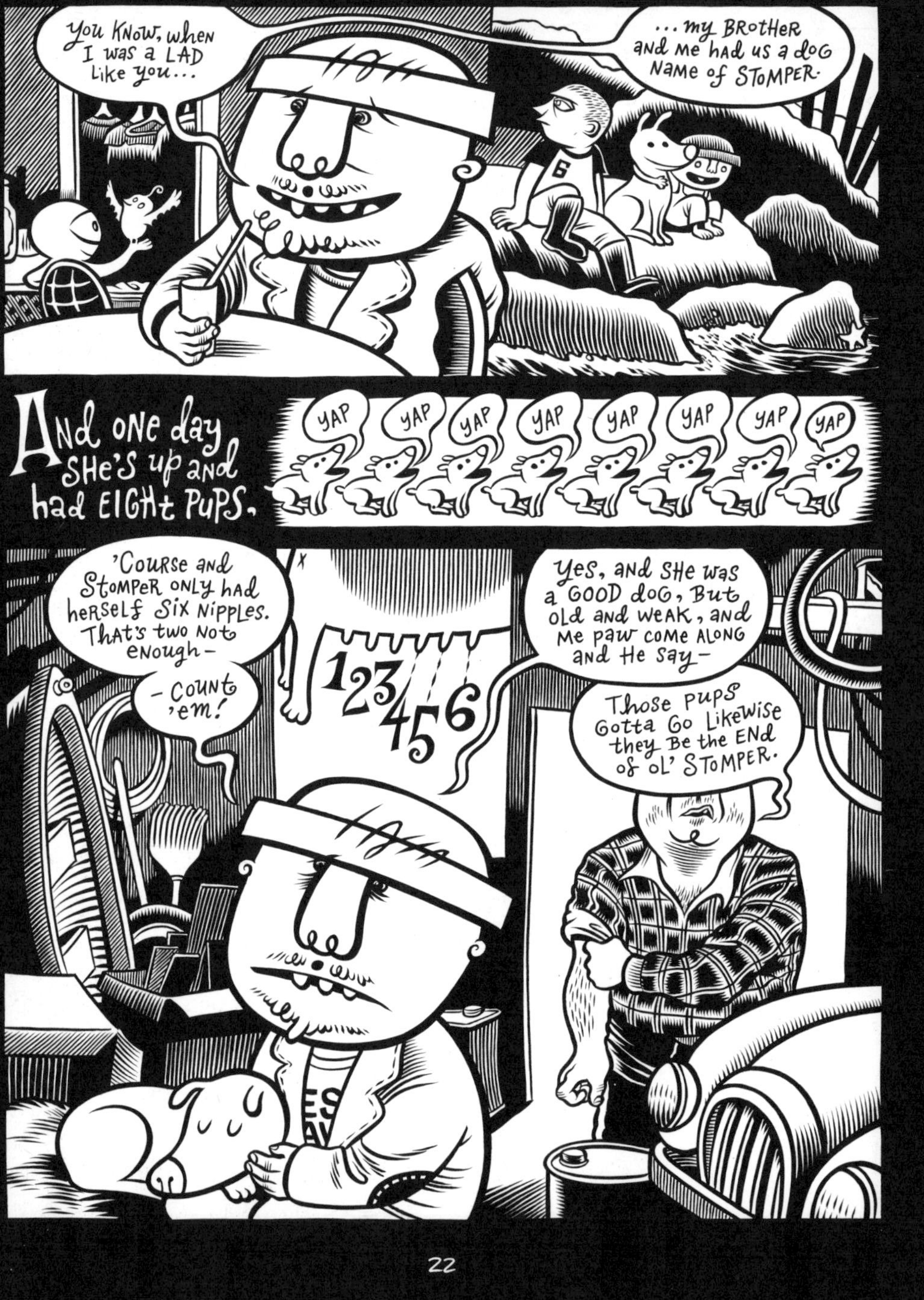
You KNOW, when I was a LAD Like you...
...my BROTHER and me had us a dog NAME of STOMPER.
And one day SHE'S up and had EIGHt PUPS.
YAP YAP YAP YAP YAP YAP YAP YAP
'Course and Stomper ONLY had herself SIX NIPPLES. That's two Not enough-
-Count 'em!
1 2 3 4 5 6
Yes, and SHE was a GOOD dog, But old and WEAK, and me paw come ALONG and He say-
Those PUPS Gotta Go Likewise they Be the END of oL' STOMPER.

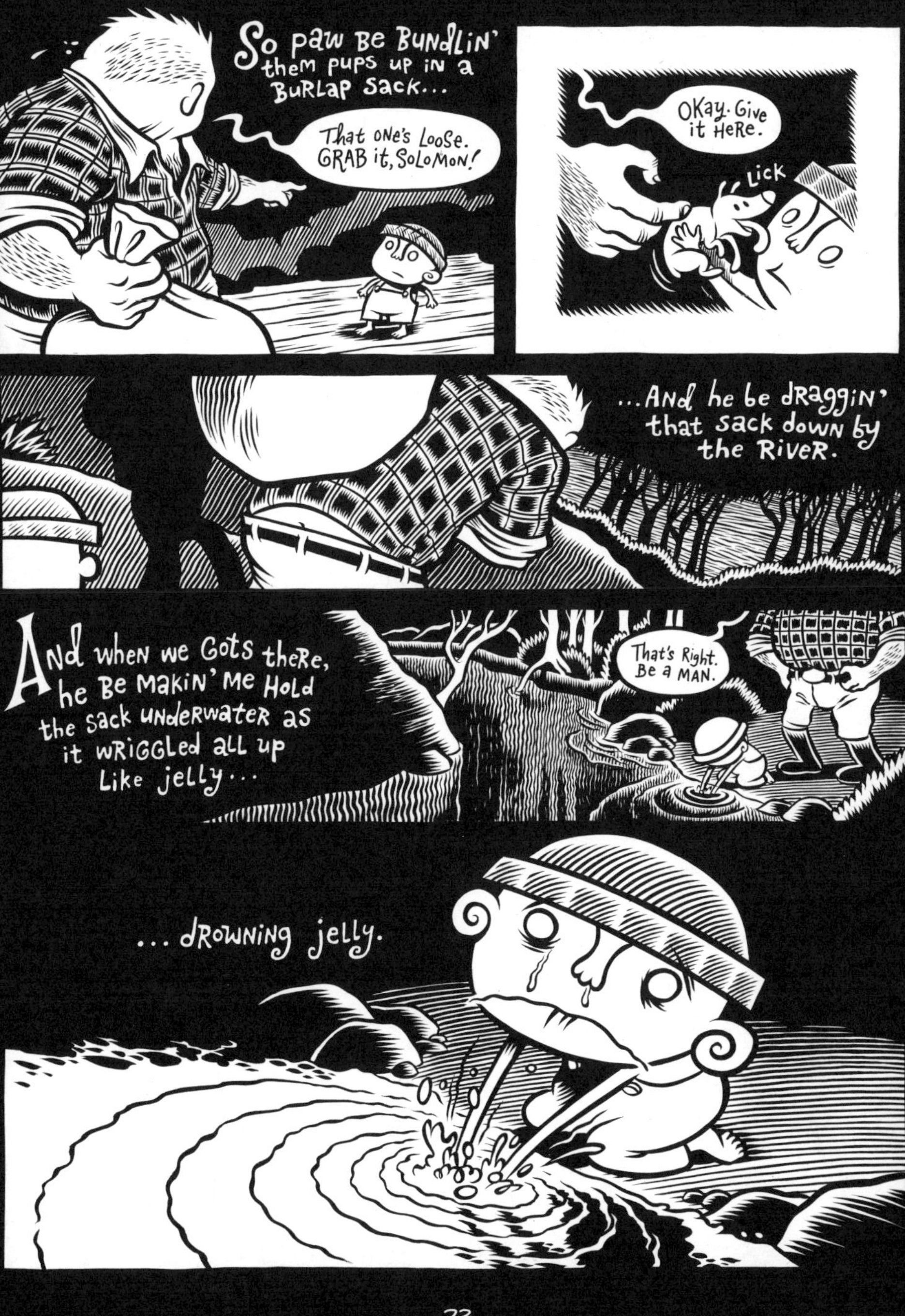
So paw be bundlin' them pups up in a burlap sack...
That one's loose. Grab it, Solomon!
Okay. Give it here.
Lick
...And he be draggin' that sack down by the river.
And when we gots there, he be makin' me hold the sack underwater as it wriggled all up like jelly...
That's right. Be a man.
...drowning jelly.

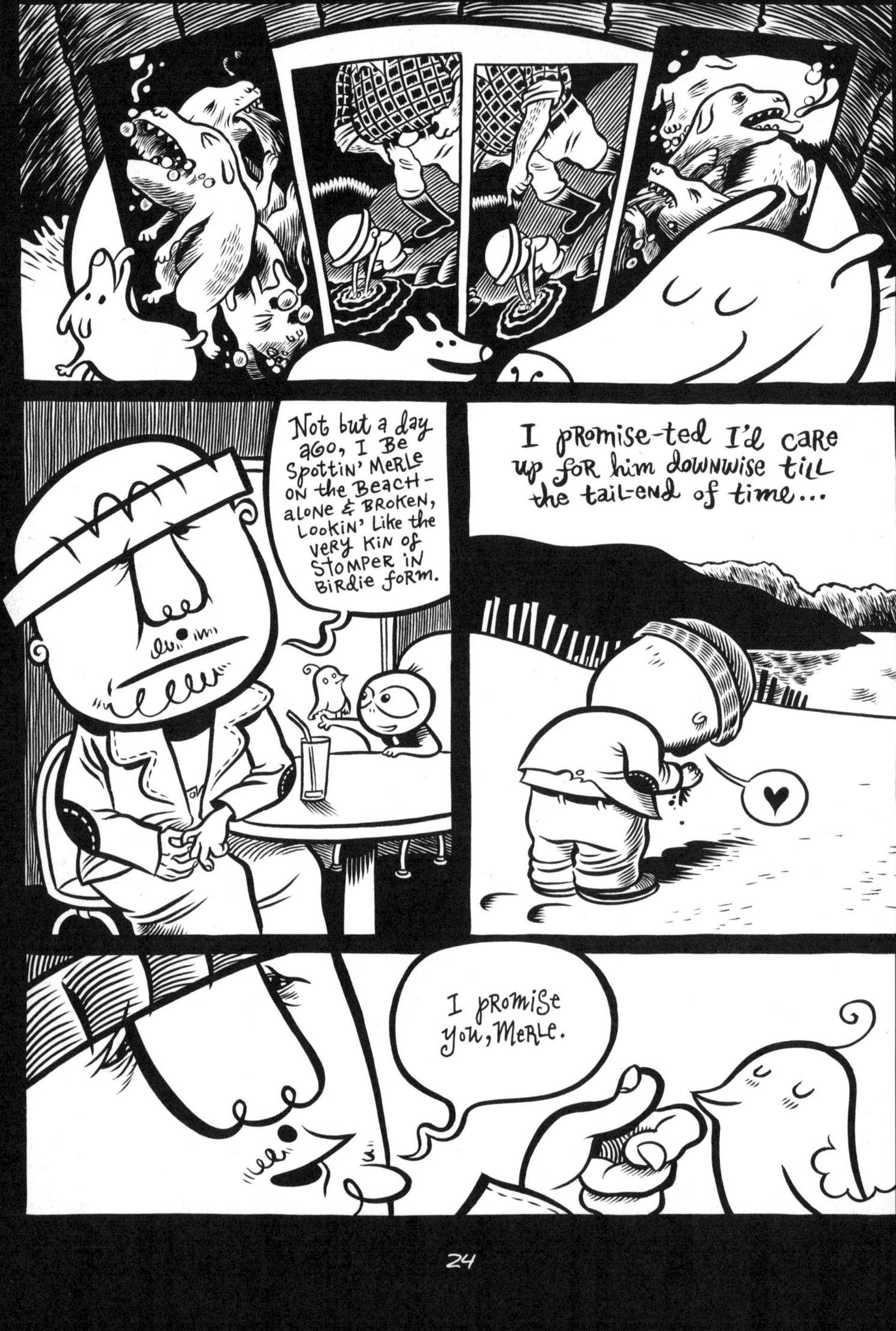
Not but a day ago, I Be Spottin' Merle on the Beach - alone & Broken, Lookin' Like the very Kin of Stomper in Birdie form.
I promise-ted I'd care up for him downwise till the tail-end of time...
I promise you, Merle.

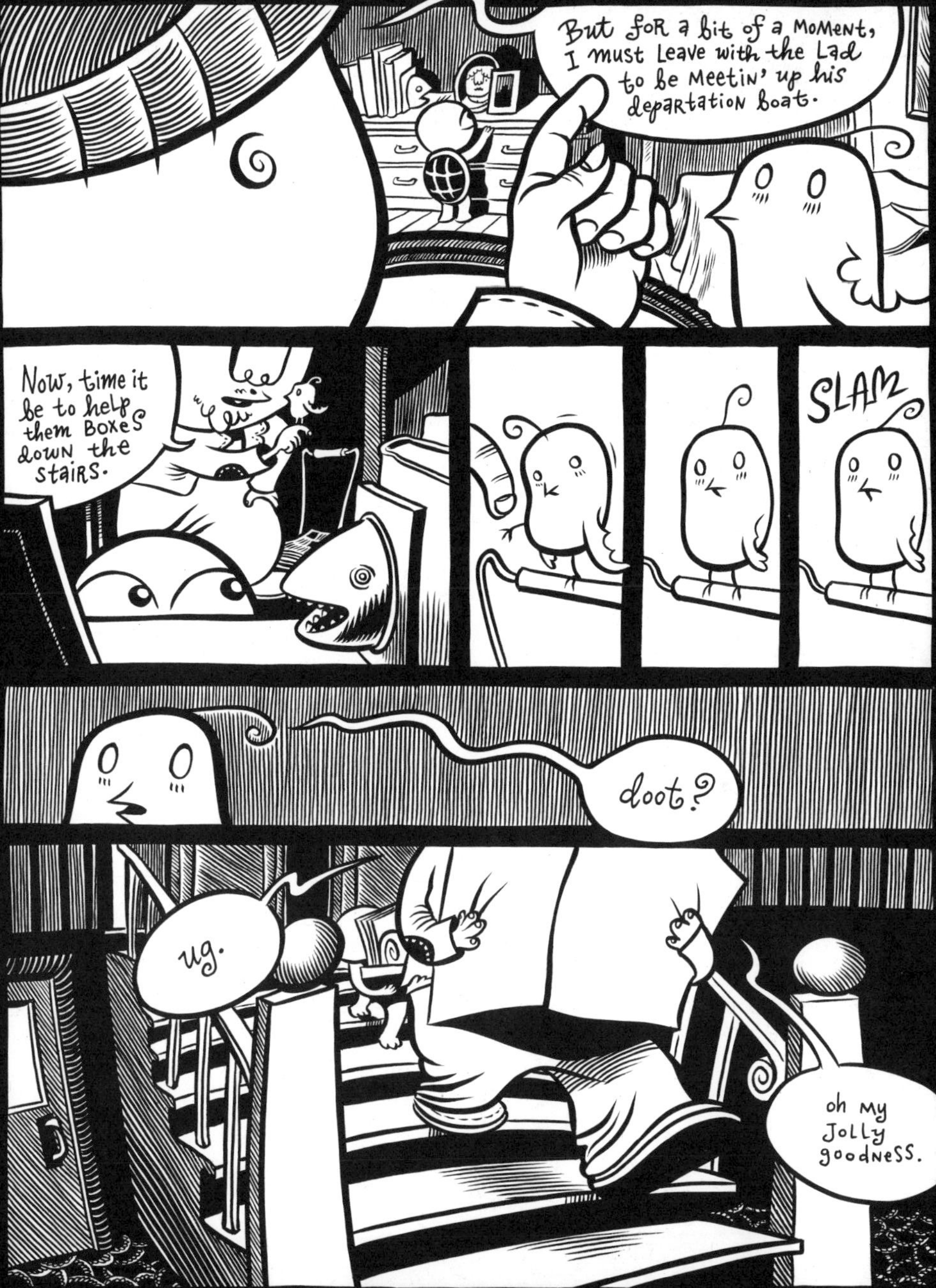
But for a bit of a moment, I must leave with the Lad to be meetin' up his departation boat.
Now, time it be to help them boxes down the stairs.
SLAM
doot?
ug.
oh my jolly goodness.

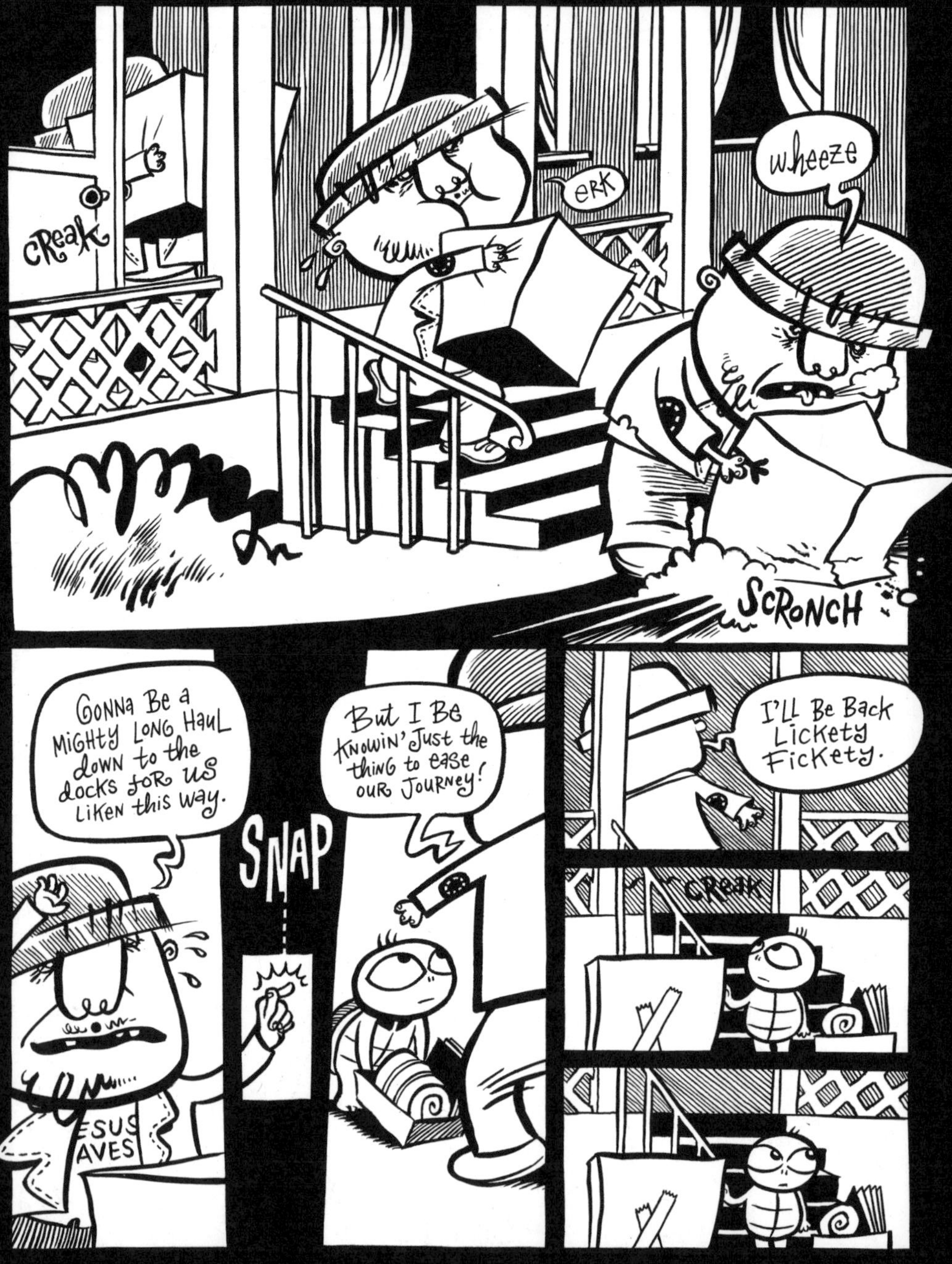

Creak
erk
wheeze
SCRONCH
Gonna Be a Mighty Long Haul down to the docks for us liken this way.
SNAP
But I Be knowin' just the thing to ease our journey!
I'll Be Back Lickety Fickety.
Creak
ESUS AVES

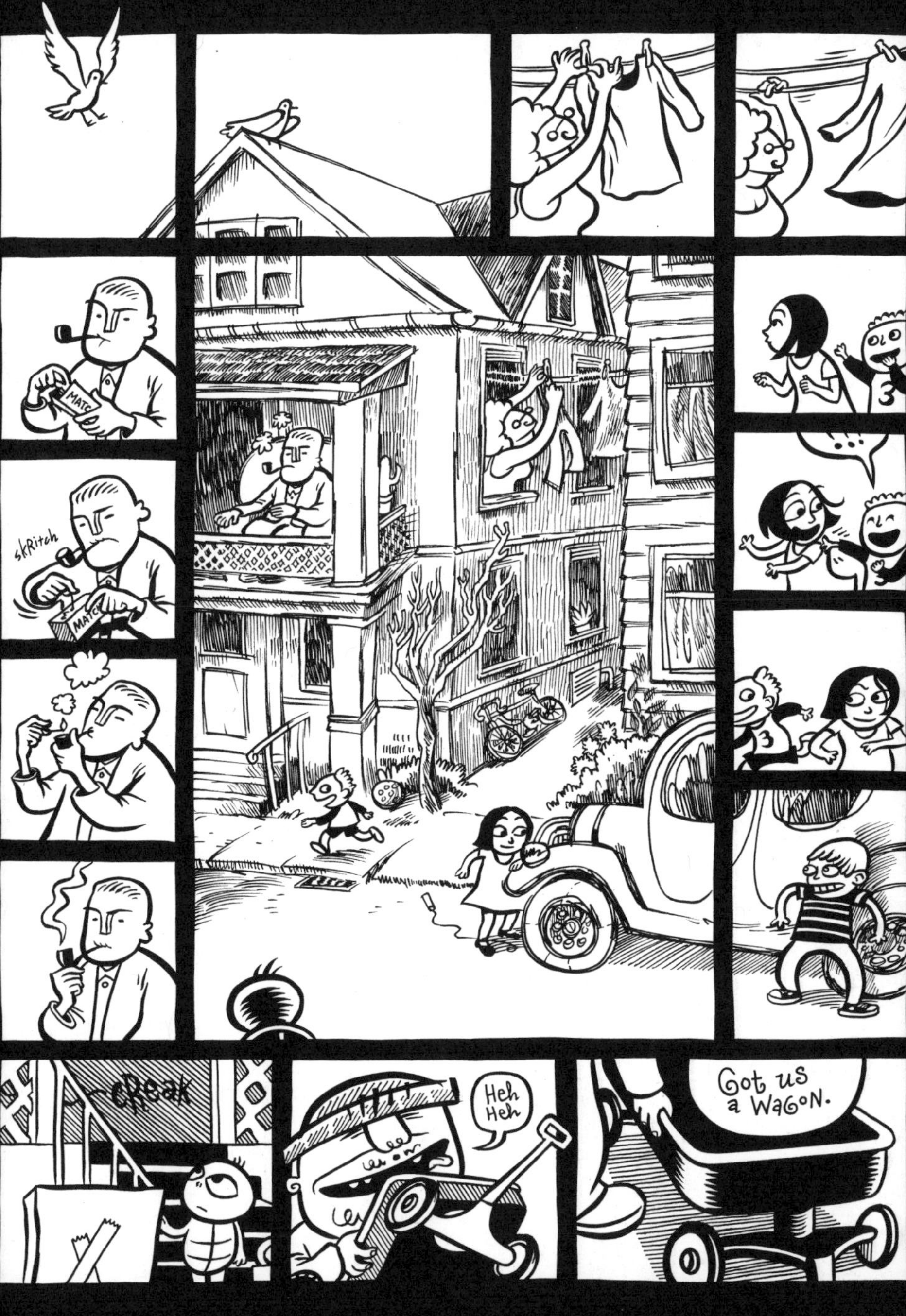
MATCH
skRitch
MATCH
cReak
Heh Heh
Got us a WaGoN.

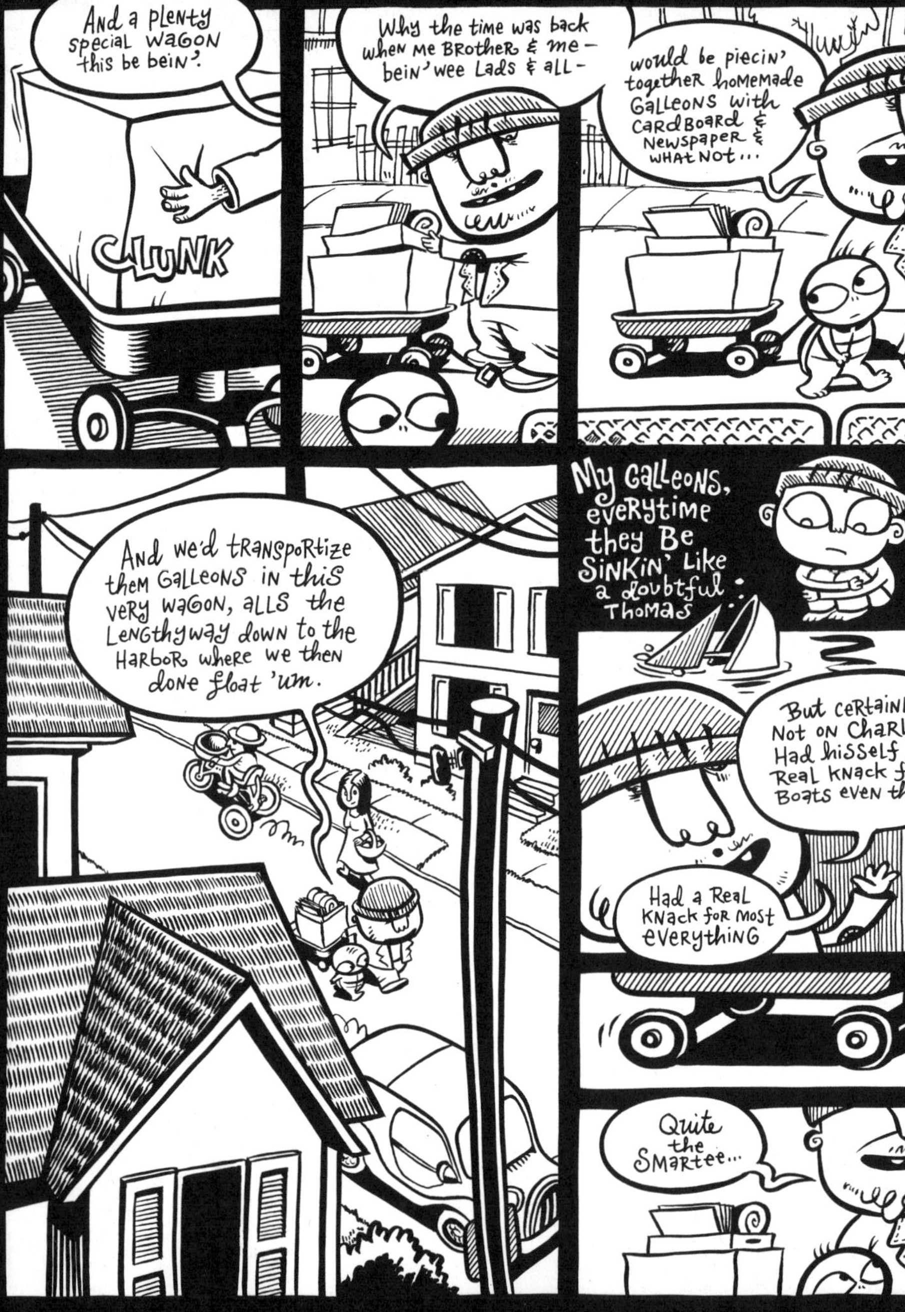

And a plenty special wagon this be bein'.
CLUNK
Why the time was back when me brother & me - bein' wee lads & all -
would be piecin' together homemade galleons with cardboard & newspaper & whatnot...
And we'd transportize them galleons in this very wagon, alls the lengthyway down to the harbor where we then done float 'um.
My galleons, everytime they be sinkin' like a doubtful Thomas
But certainly not on Charles. Had hisself a real knack for boats even then.
Had a real knack for most everything
Quite the smartee...

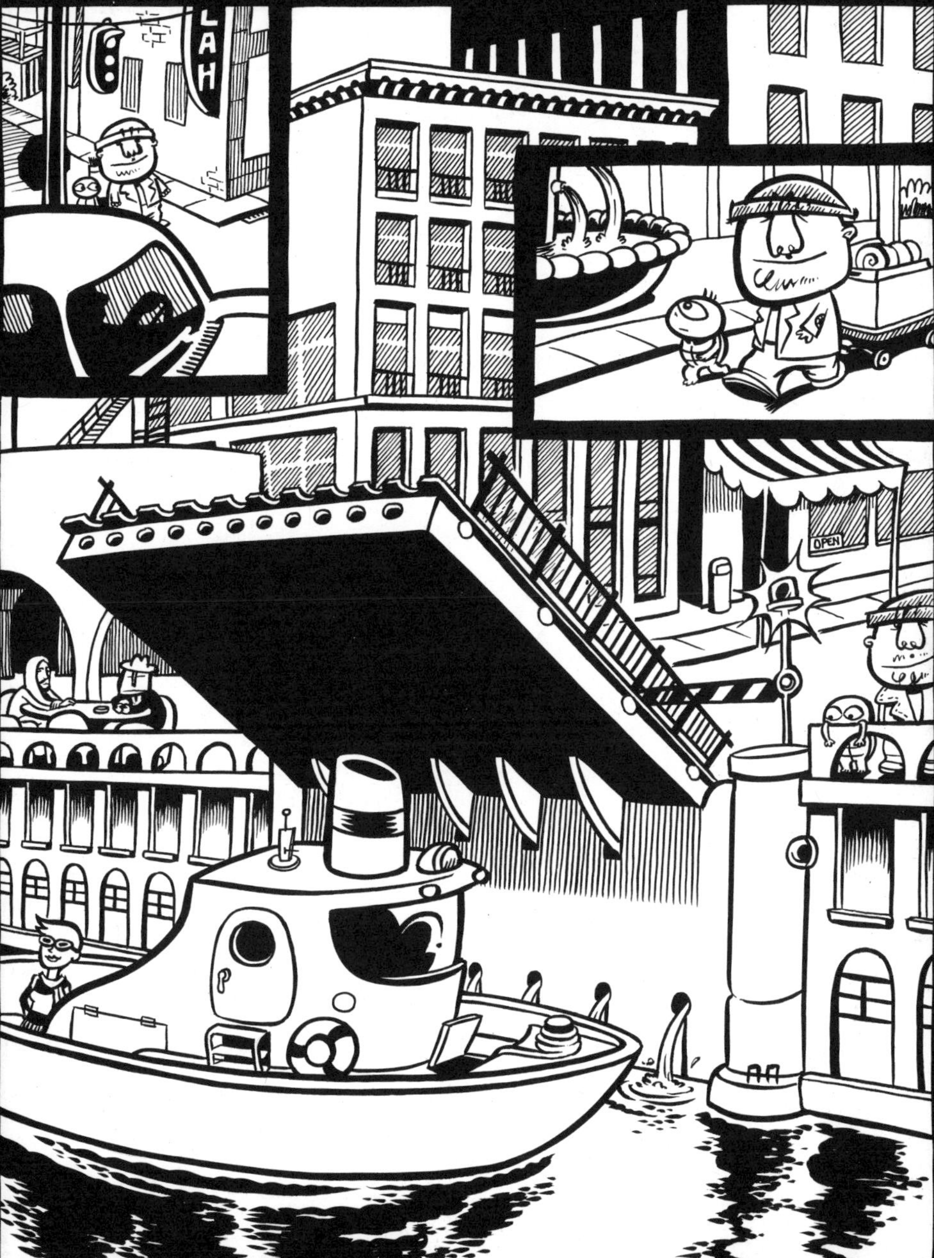
LAH
OPEN

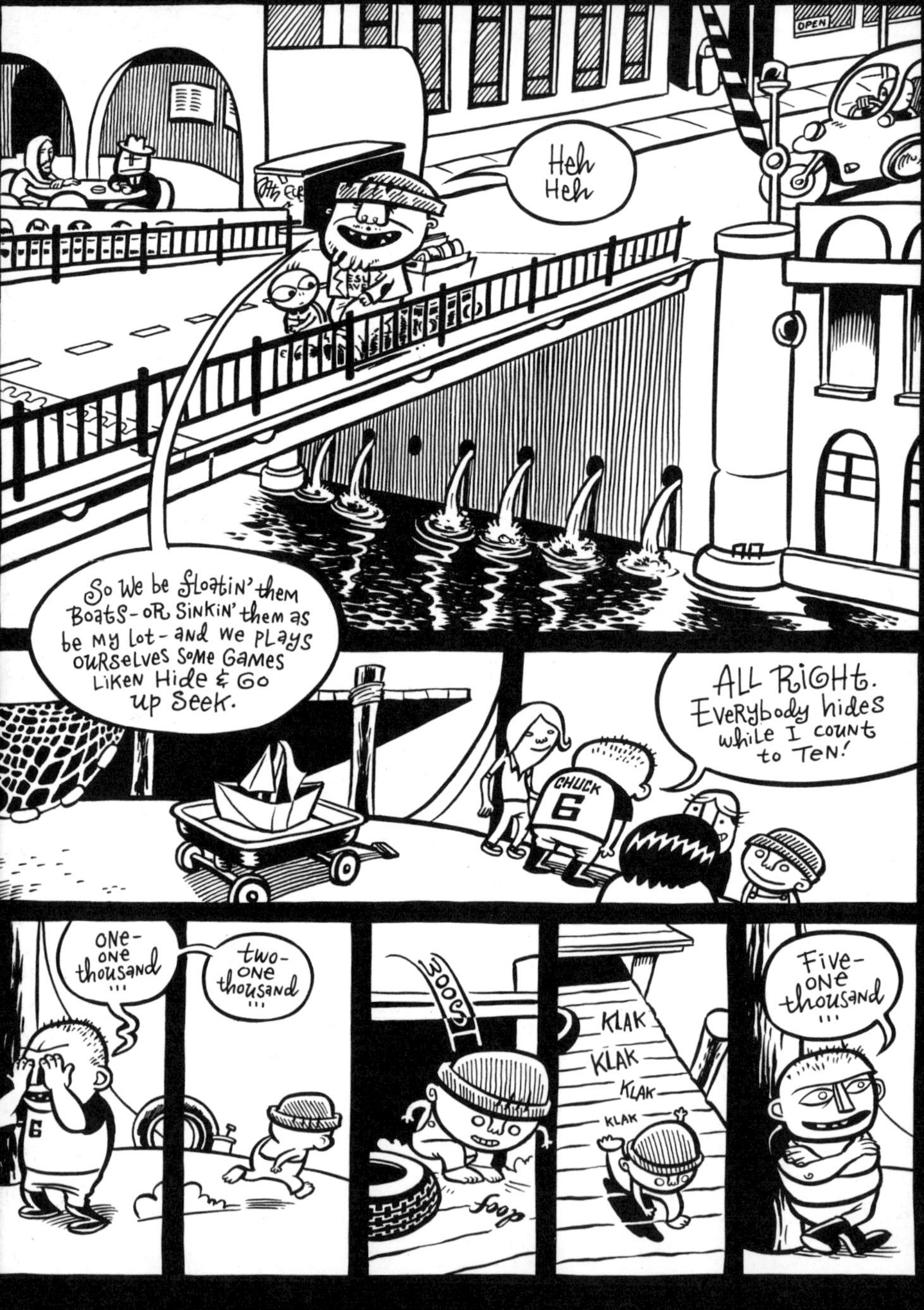
Heh Heh
So We be floatin' them Boats - oR Sinkin' them as be my lot - and we plays ourselves some Games liken Hide & Go up Seek.
ALL RiGHt. Everybody hides while I count to TEN!
CHUCK 6
ONE-ONE thousand ...
two-ONE thousand ...
SWOOSH
foop
KLAK KLAK KLAK KLAK
Five-ONE thousand ...

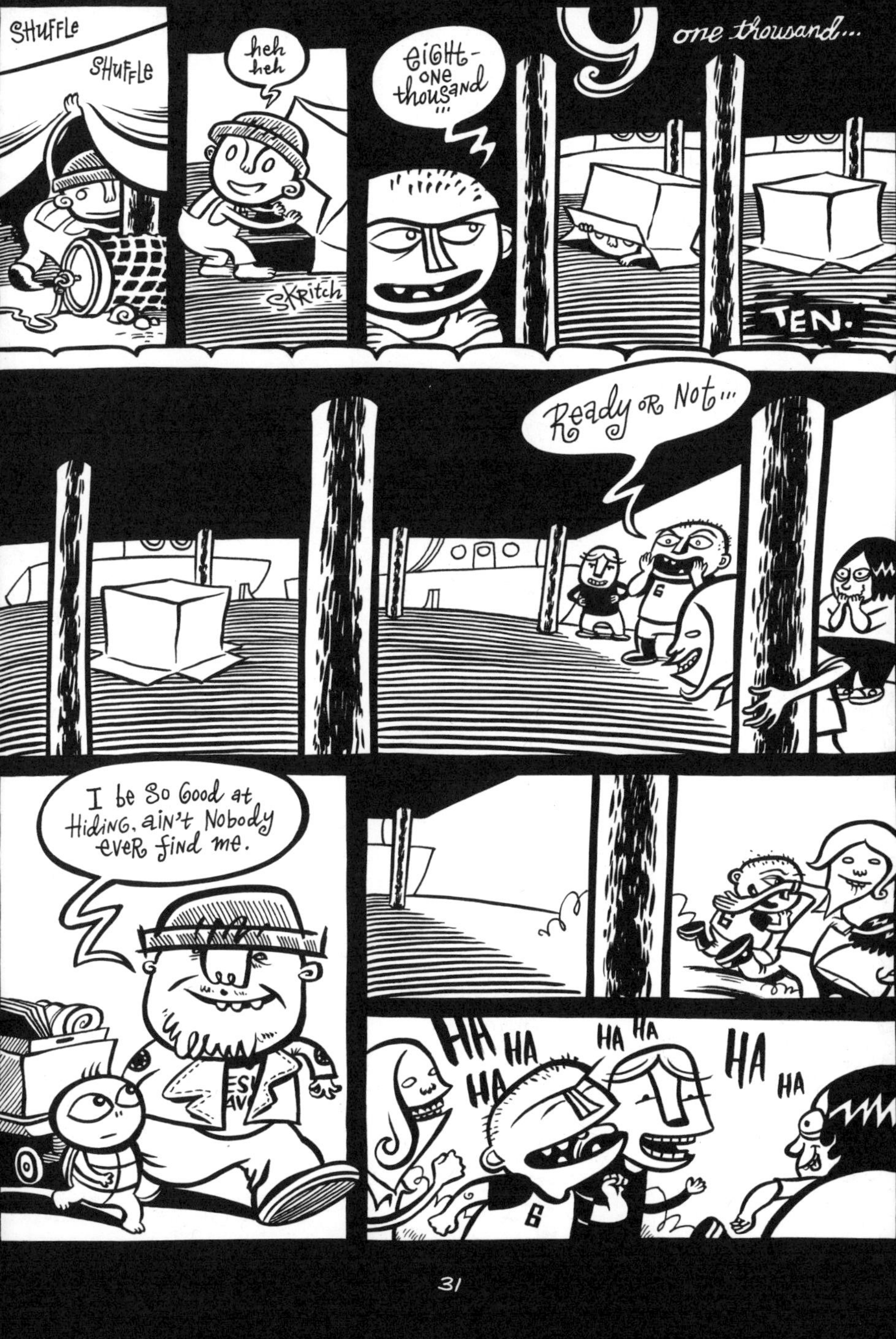
SHUFFLE
SHUFFLE
heh heh
SKRITCH
EIGHT-ONE THOUSAND ...
9 one thousand...
TEN.
Ready OR Not...
I be So Good at Hiding. ain't Nobody ever find me.
HA HA HA HA HA HA HA HA

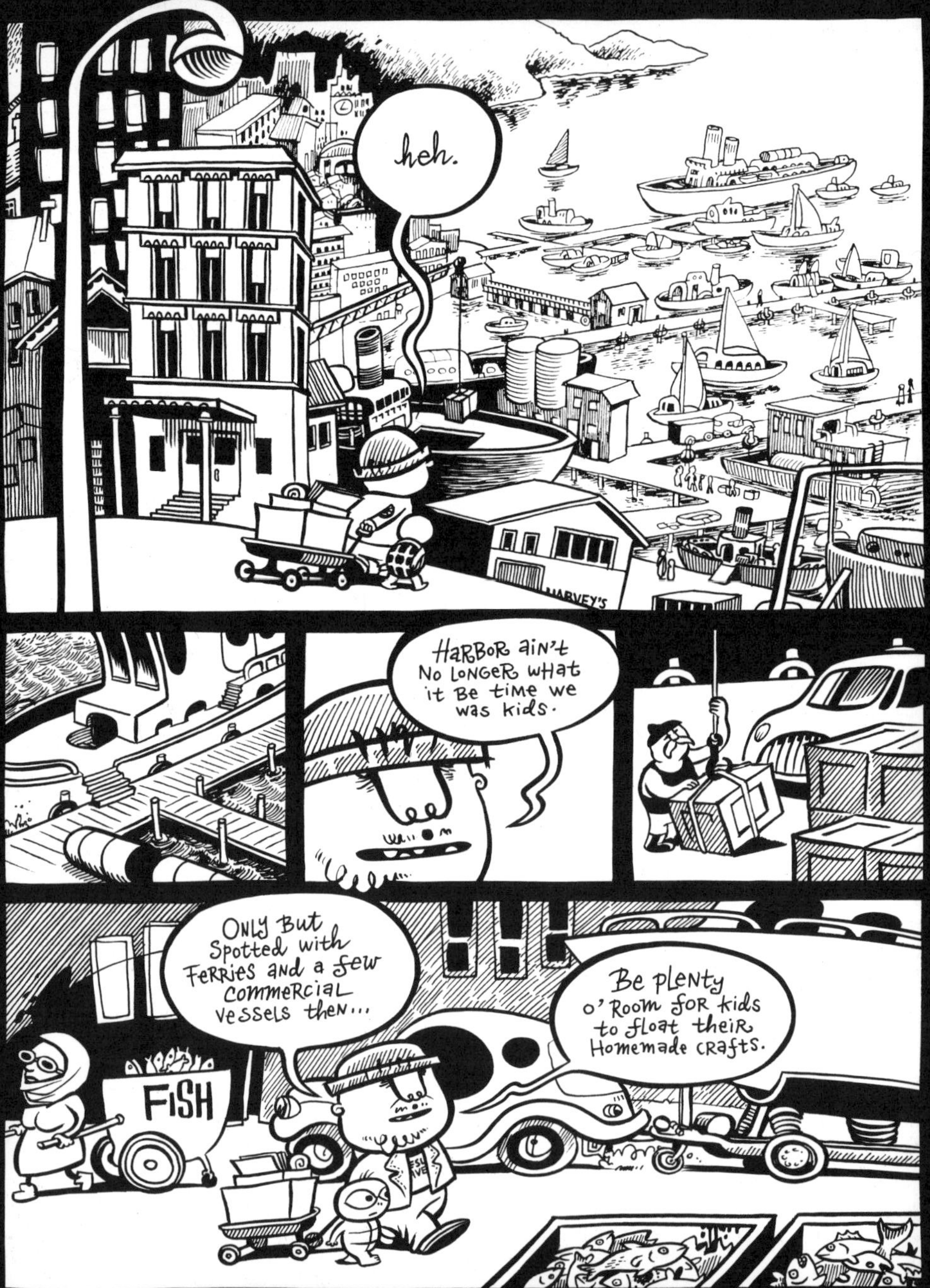
heh.
HARVEY'S
HARBOR ain't No LONGER WHAT it Be time we was kids.
ONLY But Spotted with Ferries and a few commercial vessels then...
Be plenty o' Room for kids to float their Homemade crafts.
FISH

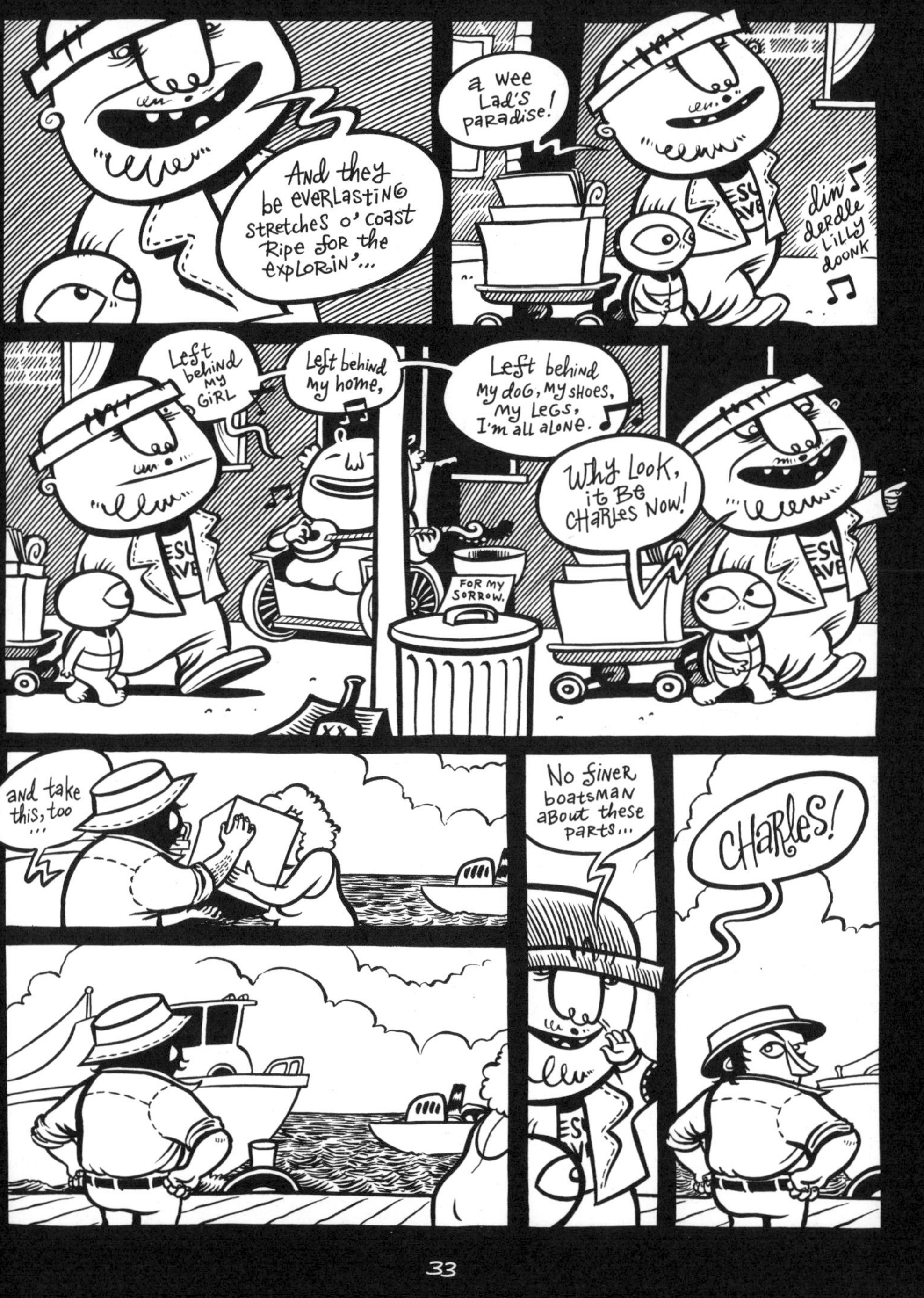
And they be everlasting stretches o' coast ripe for the explorin'...
a wee Lad's paradise!
dim derdle lilly doonk
Left behind my girl
Left behind my home,
Left behind my dog, my shoes, my legs, I'm all alone.
Why look, it be Charles now!
FOR MY SORROW.
and take this, too...
No finer boatsman about these parts...
CHARLES!

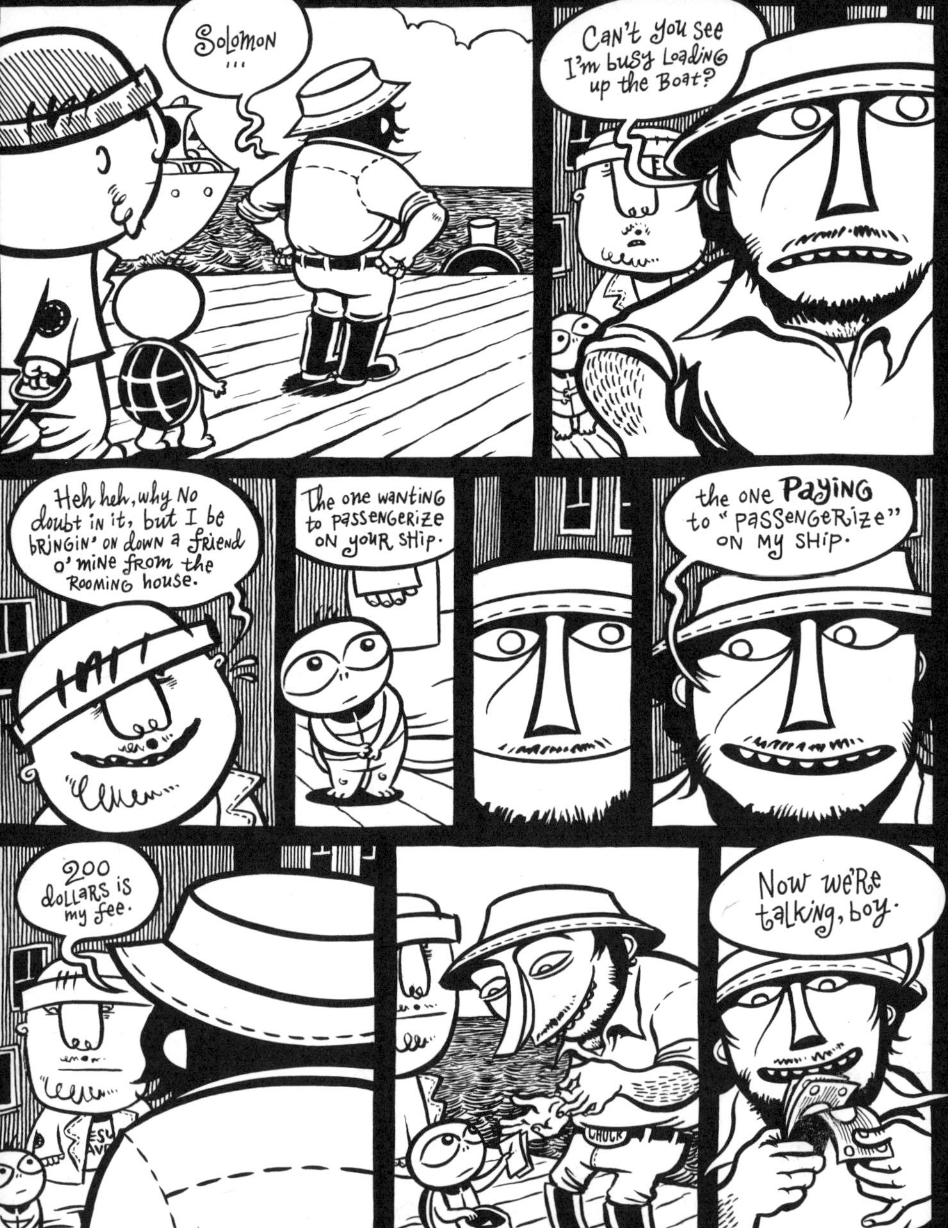
Solomon ...
Can't you see I'm busy loading up the Boat?
Heh heh, why no doubt in it, but I be bringin' on down a friend o' mine from the rooming house.
The one wanting to passengerize on your ship.
the one Paying to "passengerize" on my ship.
200 dollars is my fee.
CHUCK
Now we're talking, boy.
CHUCK

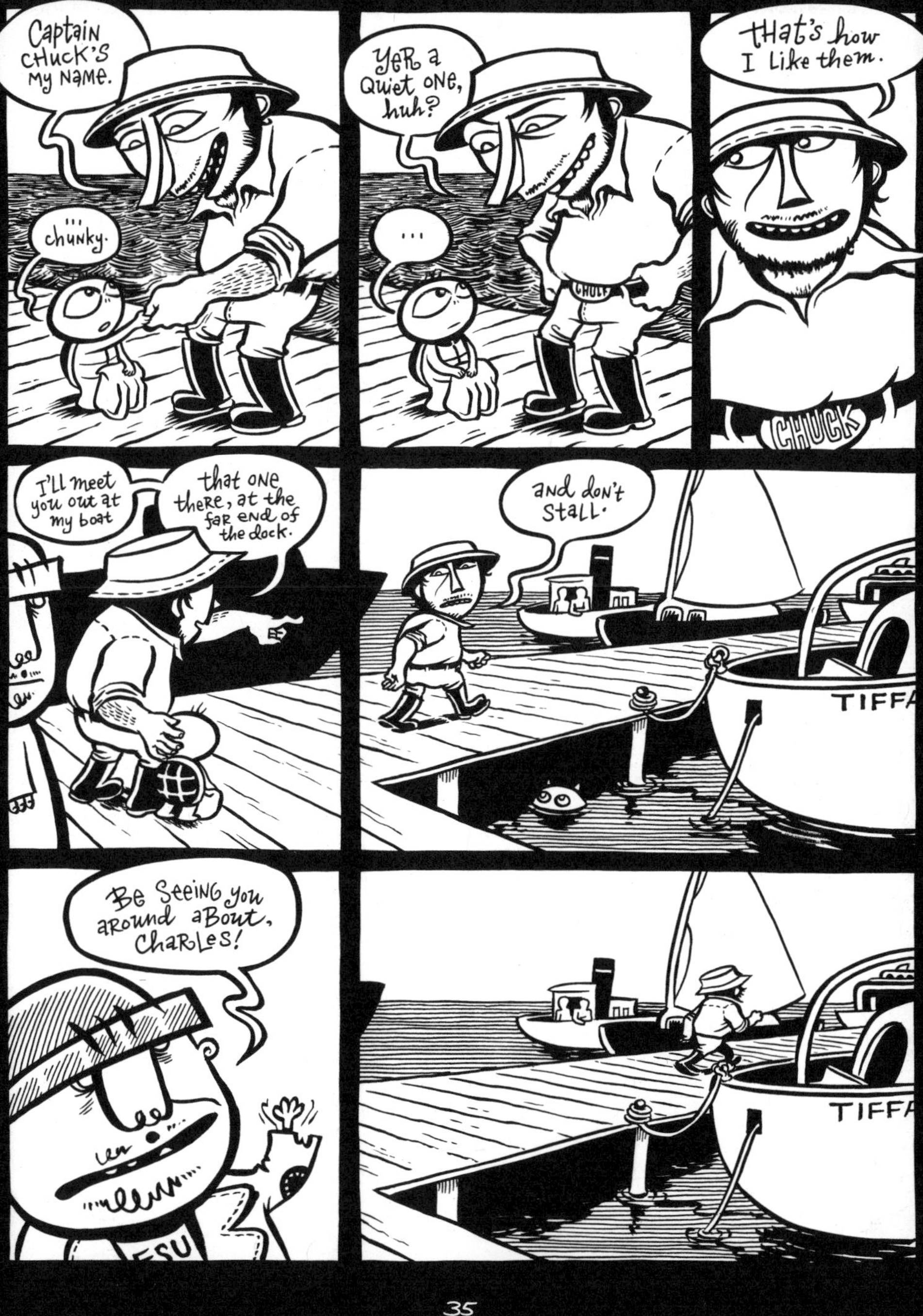
Captain Chuck's my name.
... chunky.
Yer a quiet one, huh?
...
CHUCK
That's how I like them.
CHUCK
I'll meet you out at my boat
that one there, at the far end of the dock.
and don't stall.
TIFFA
Be seeing you around about, Charles!
FSU
TIFFA

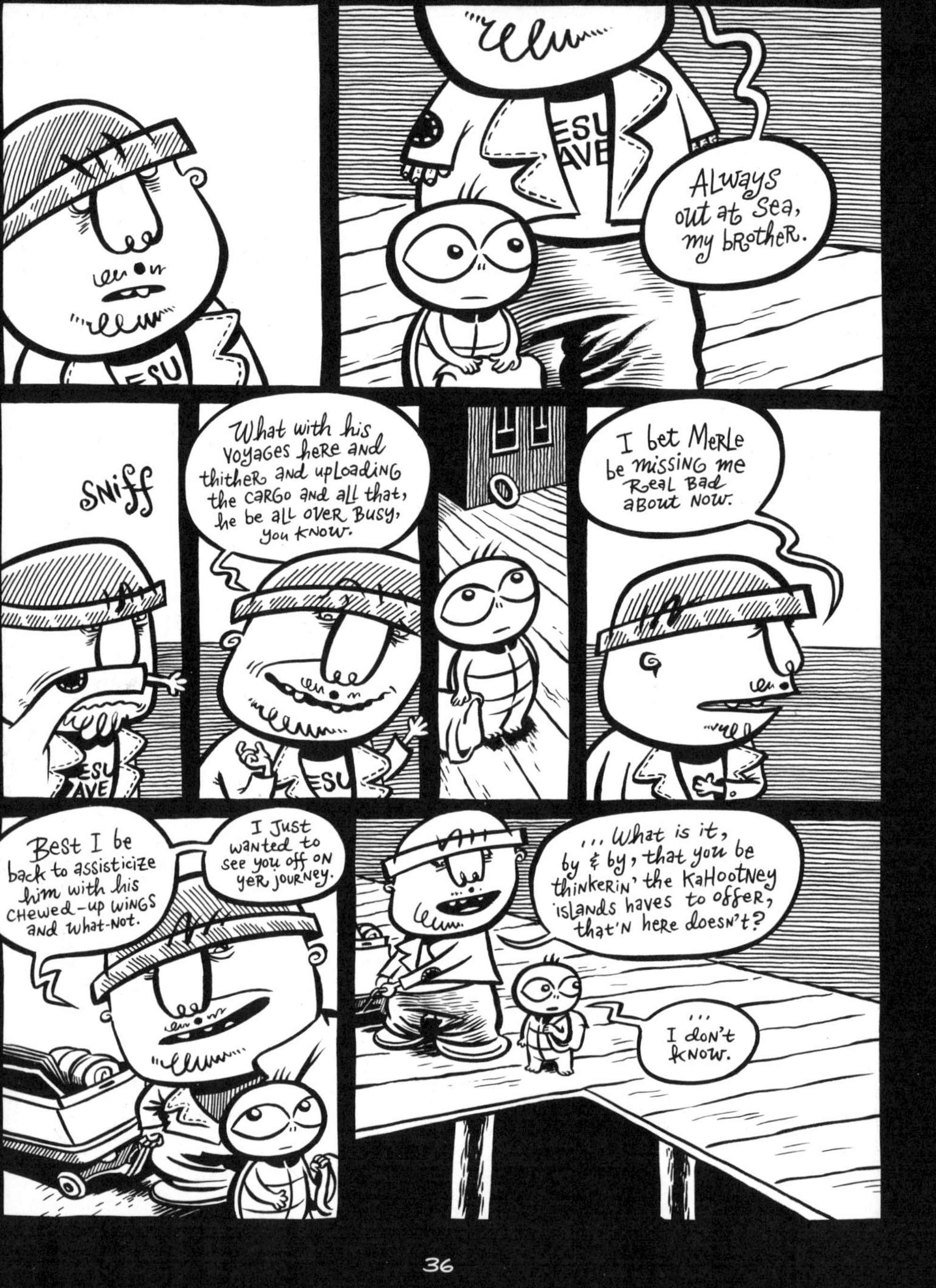
Always out at sea, my brother.
SNIFF
What with his voyages here and thither and uploading the cargo and all that, he be all over busy, you know.
I bet Merle be missing me real bad about now.
Best I be back to assisticize him with his chewed-up wings and what-not.
I just wanted to see you off on yer journey.
...What is it, by & by, that you be thinkerin' the Kahootney islands haves to offer, that'n here doesn't?
... I don't know.

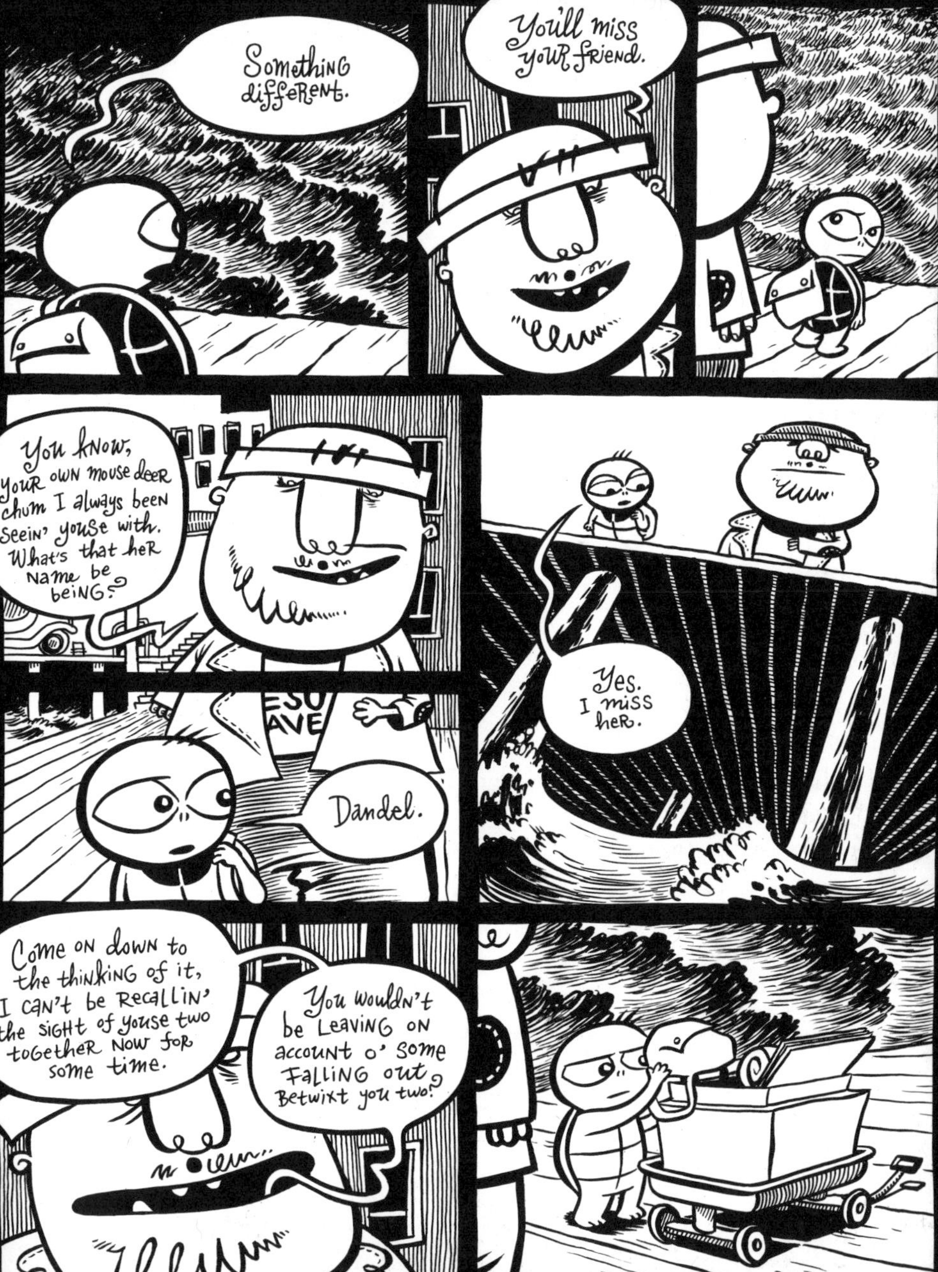
Something different.
You'll miss your friend.
You know, your own mouse deer chum I always been seein' youse with. What's that her name be being?
Dandel.
Yes. I miss her.
Come on down to the thinking of it, I can't be recallin' the sight of youse two together now for some time.
You wouldn't be leaving on account o' some falling out betwixt you two?

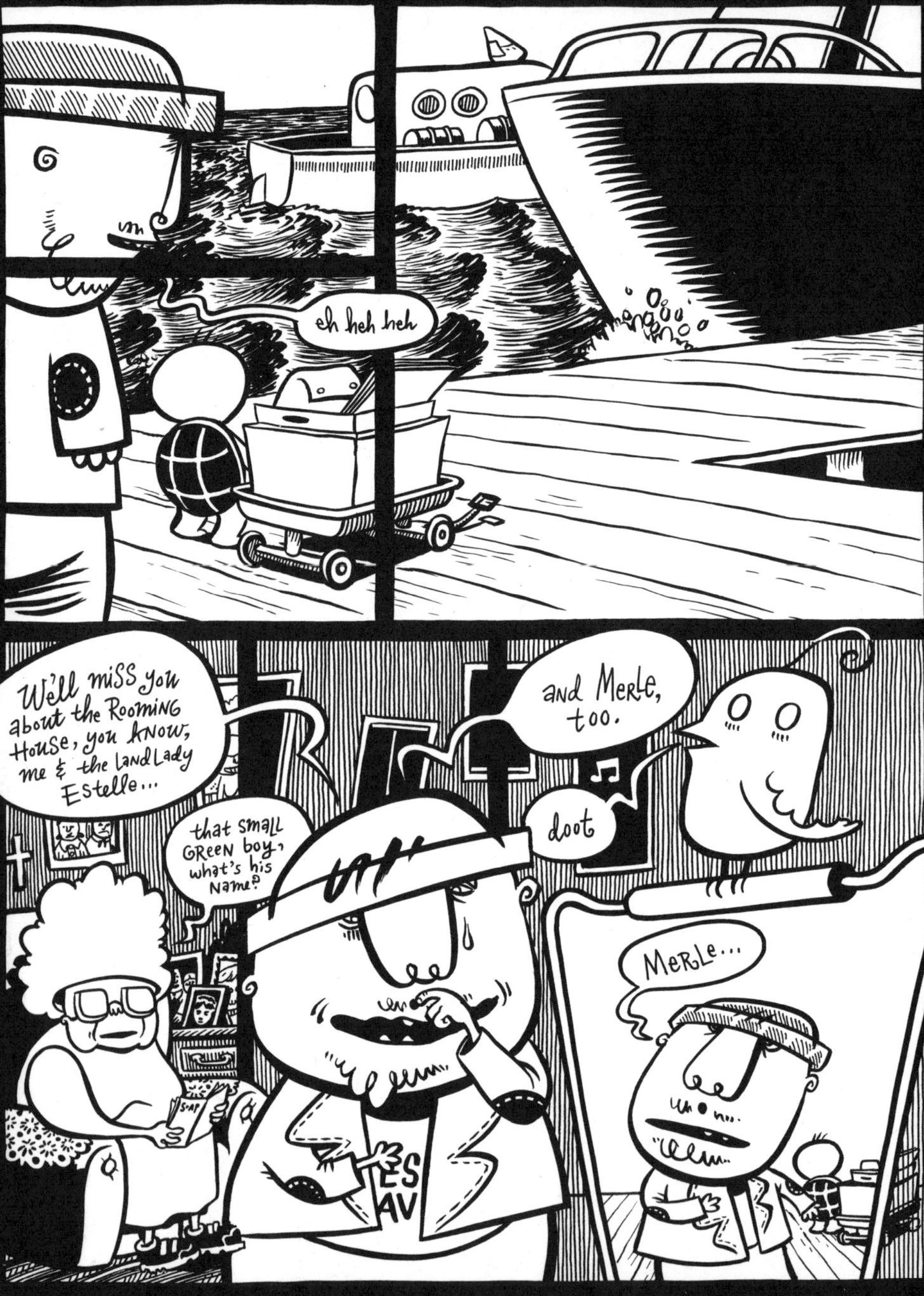
eh heh heh
We'll miss you about the Rooming House, you know, me & the landlady Estelle...
that small green boy, what's his name?
and Merle, too.
doot
Merle...

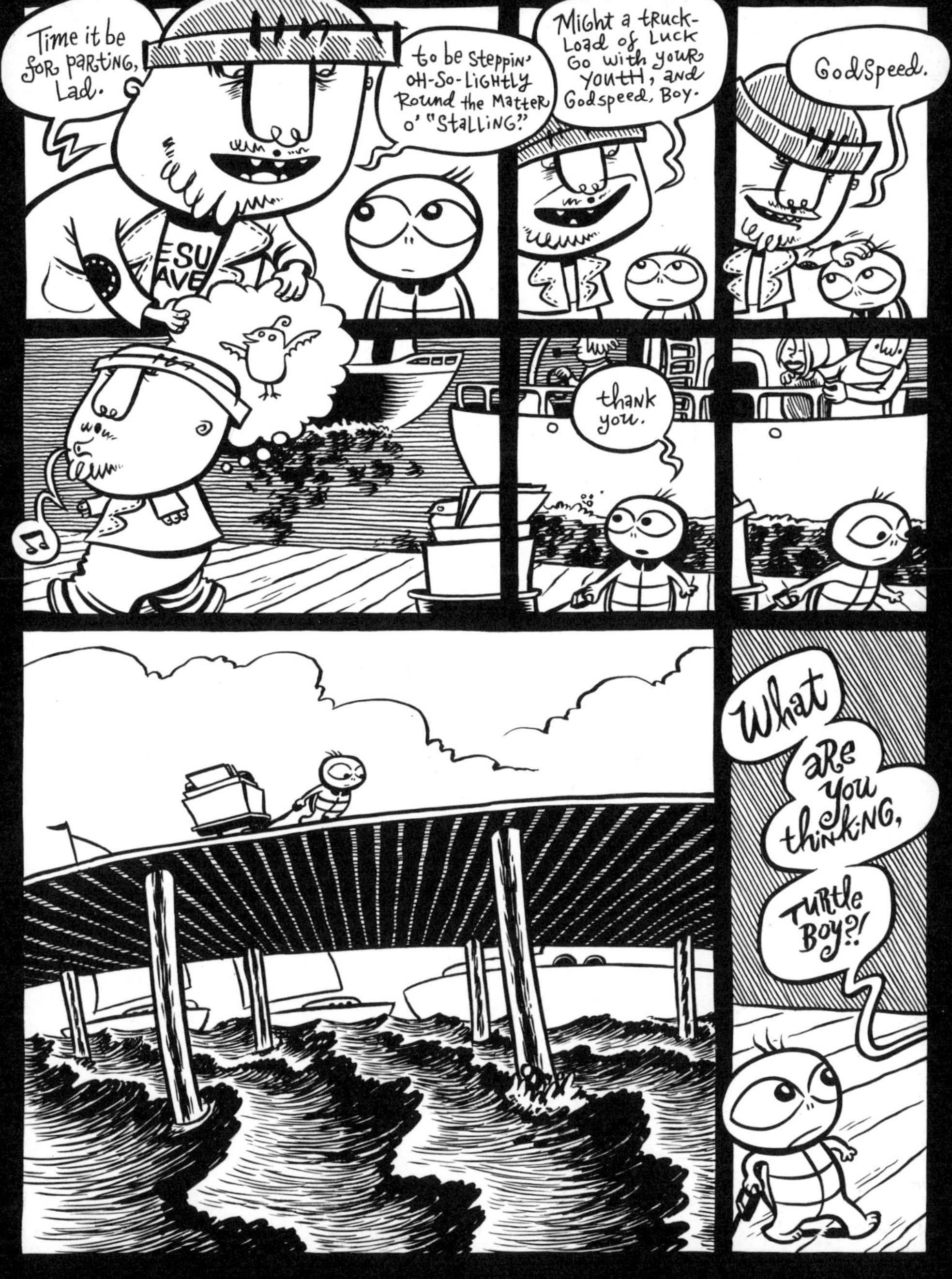
Time it be for parting, Lad.
to be steppin' oh-so-lightly Round the Matter o' "Stalling."
ESU AVE
Might a truck-Load of Luck Go with your youth, and Godspeed, Boy.
Godspeed.
thank you.
What are you thinking, Turtle Boy?!

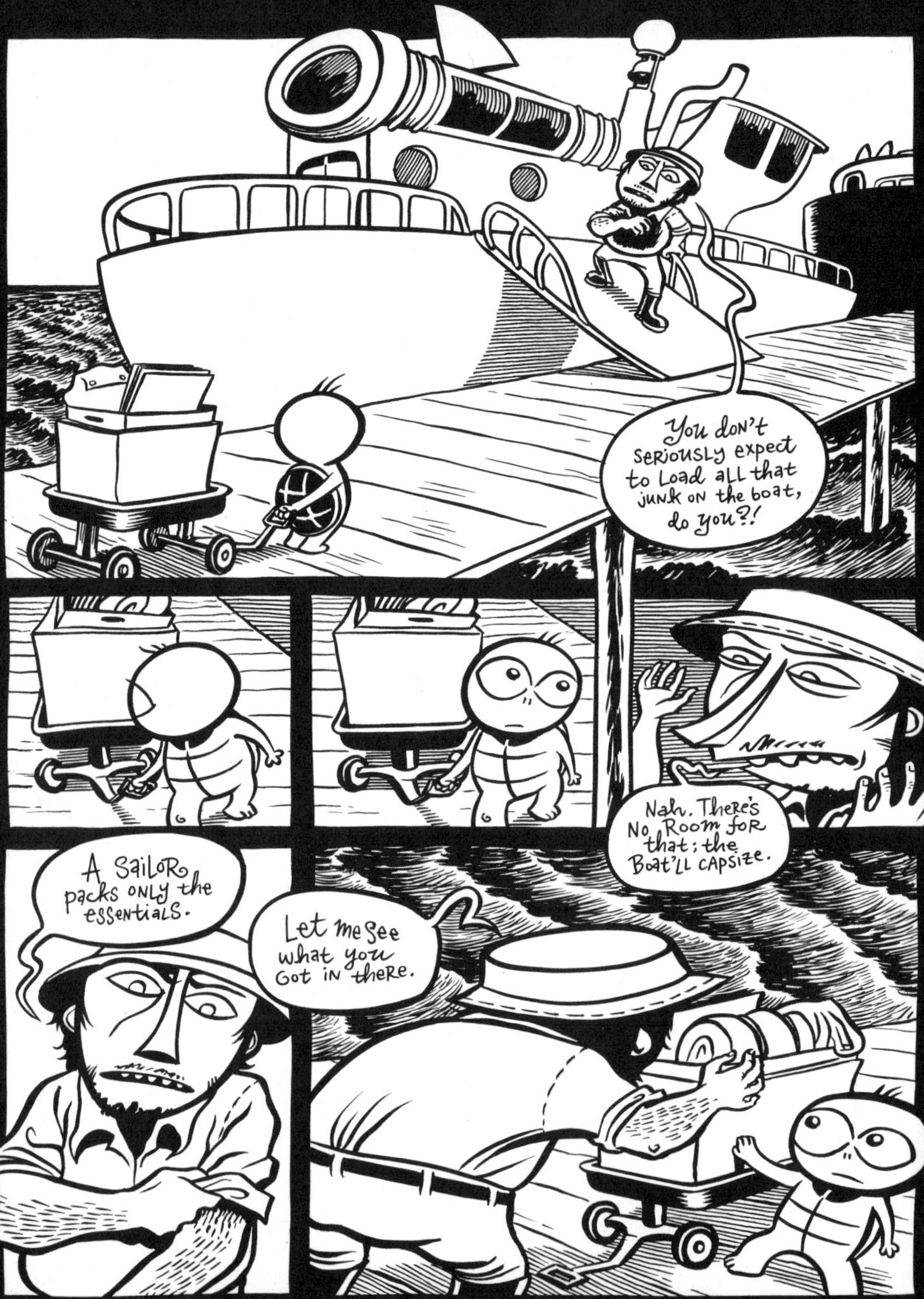
You don't seriously expect to load all that junk on the boat, do you?!
Nah. There's no room for that; the boat'll capsize.
A sailor packs only the essentials.
Let me see what you got in there.

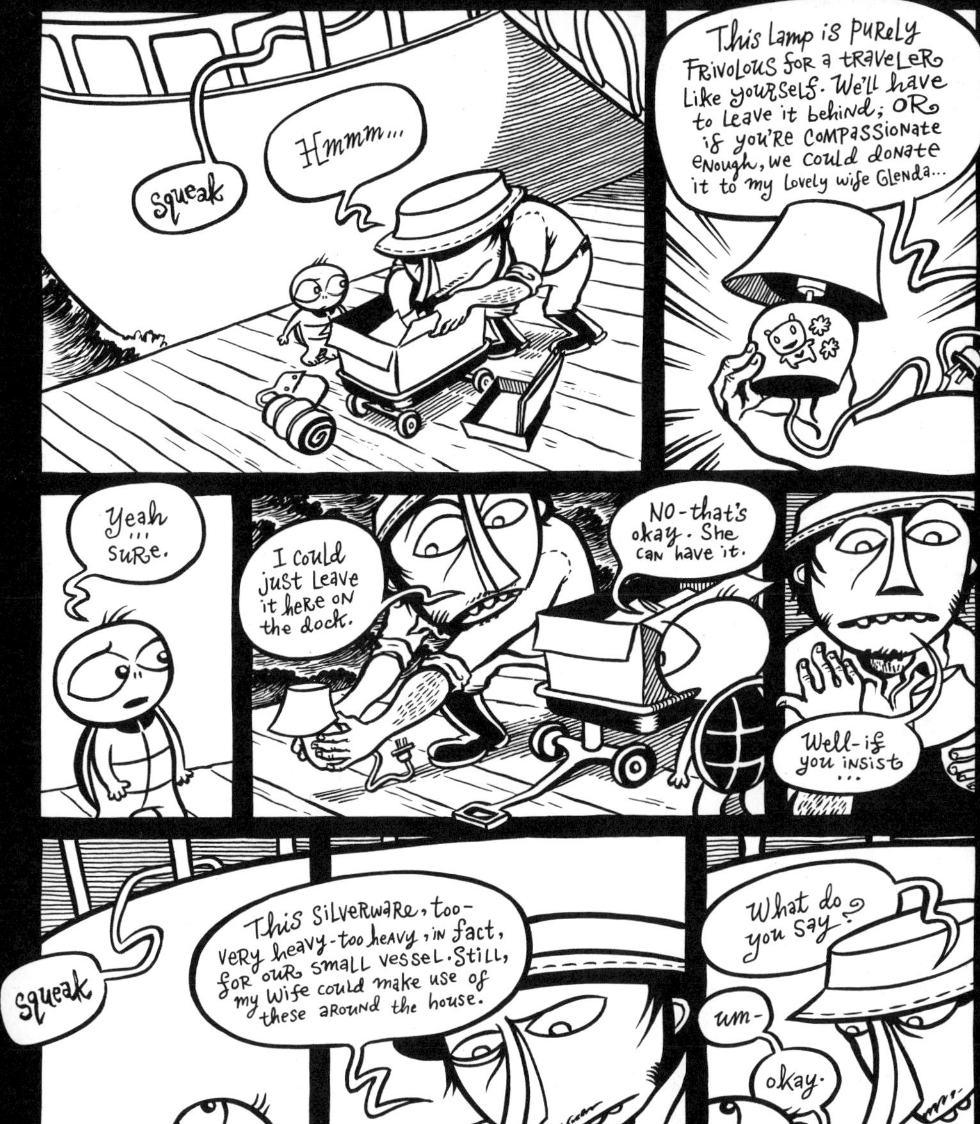
squeak
Hmmm...
This lamp is purely frivolous for a traveler like yourself. We'll have to leave it behind; or if you're compassionate enough, we could donate it to my lovely wife Glenda...
Yeah ... sure.
I could just leave it here on the dock.
No-that's okay. She can have it.
Well-if you insist ...
squeak
This silverware, too-very heavy-too heavy, in fact, for our small vessel. Still, my wife could make use of these around the house.
What do you say?
um-
okay.

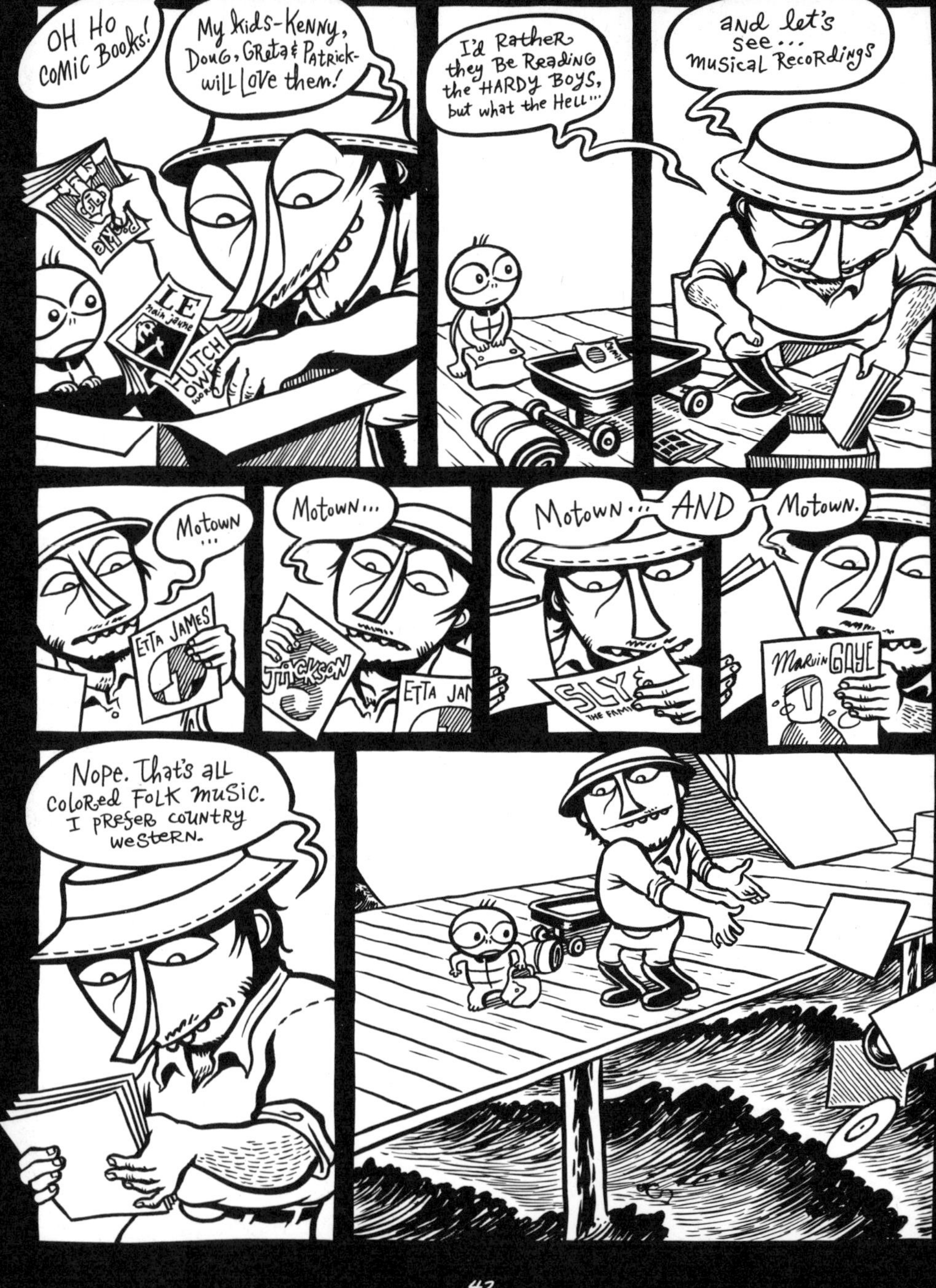

OH HO COMIC BOOKS!
My kids-Kenny, Doug, Greta & Patrick- will love them!
I'd rather they be reading the HARDY BOYS, but what the hell...
and let's see... musical recordings
Motown...
Motown...
Motown... AND Motown.
Nope. That's all colored folk music. I prefer country western.

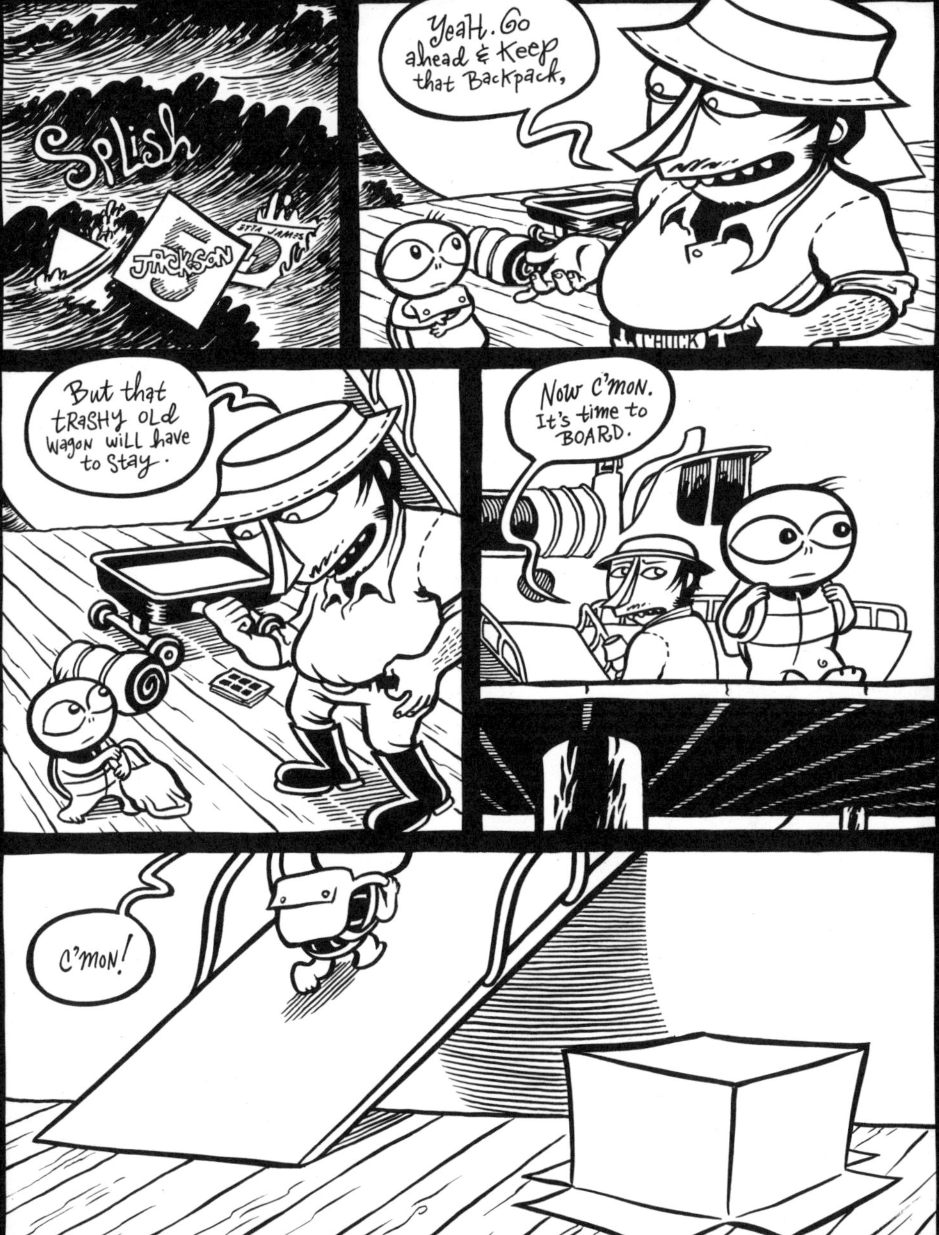
SPLISH
JACKSON 5
ETTA JAMES
YeaH. Go ahead & Keep that Backpack,
CHUCK
But that tRaSHY OLD wagon wiLL have to stay.
Now C'mon. It's time to BOARD.
C'mon!

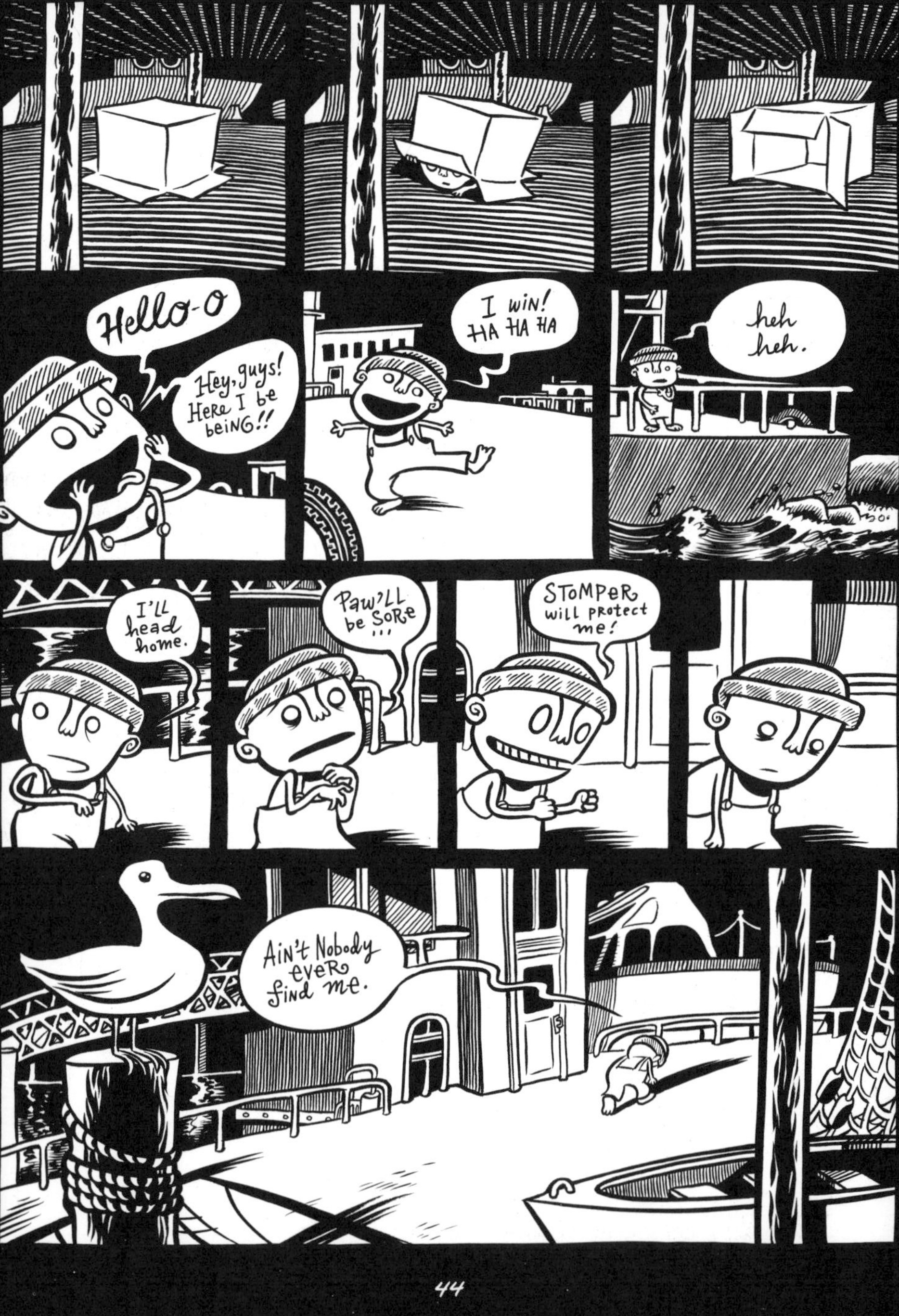
Hello-o
Hey, guys! Here I be being!!
I win! HA HA HA
heh heh.
I'll head home.
Paw'll be sore ...
Stomper will protect me!
Ain't Nobody ever find me.

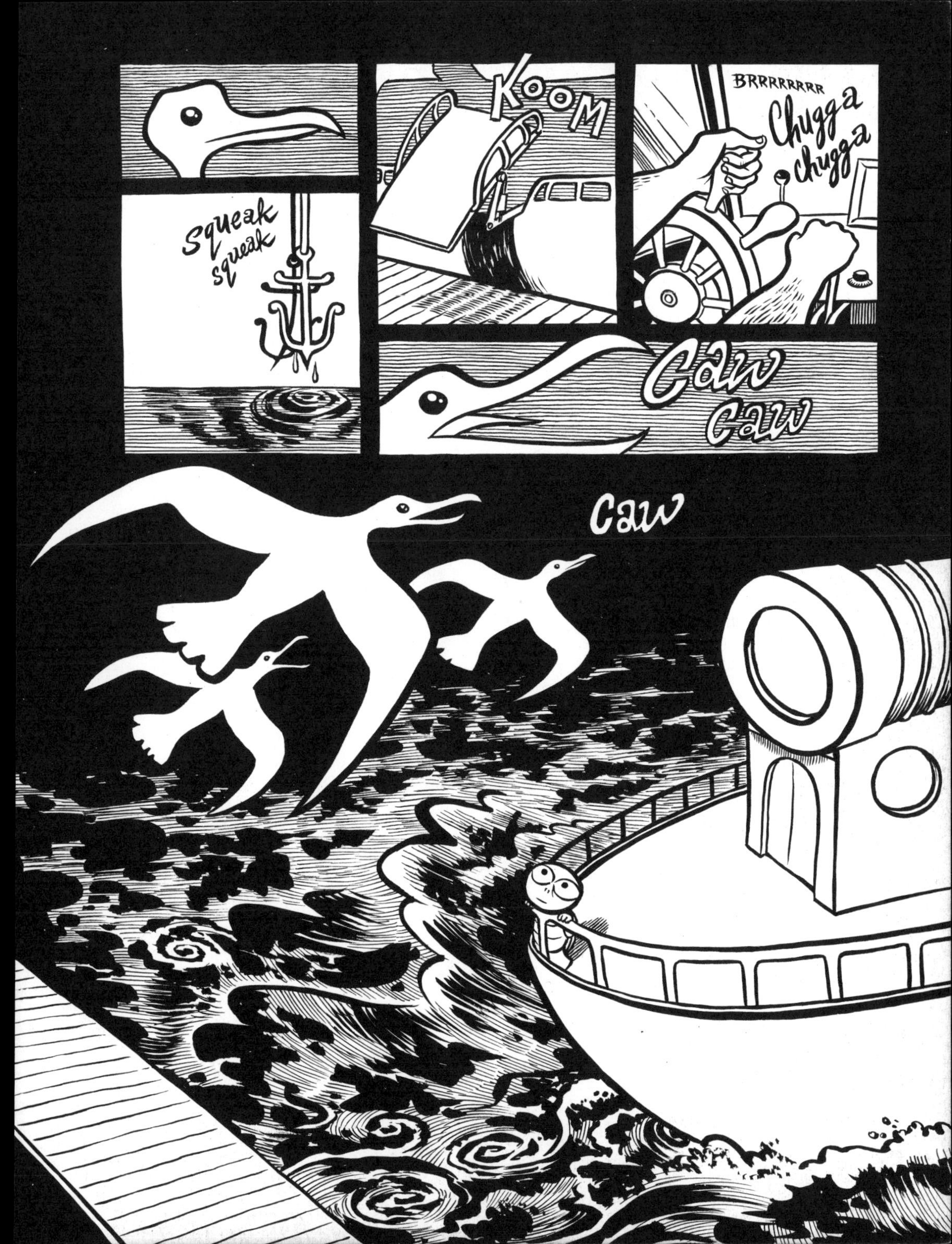
KOOM
BRRRRRRRR
Chugga chugga
squeak squeak
Caw caw
Caw

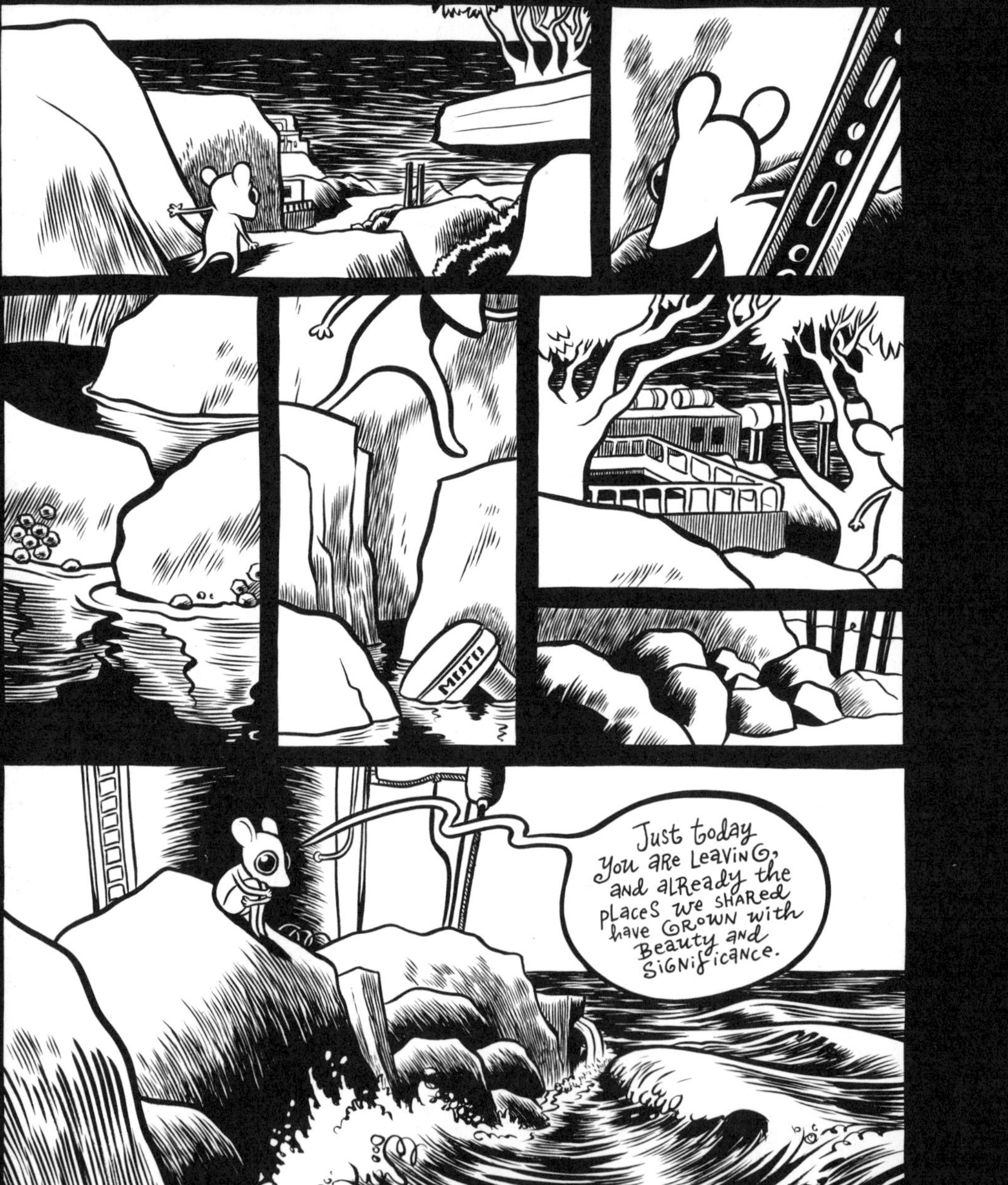
Just today you are leaving, and already the places we shared have grown with beauty and significance.

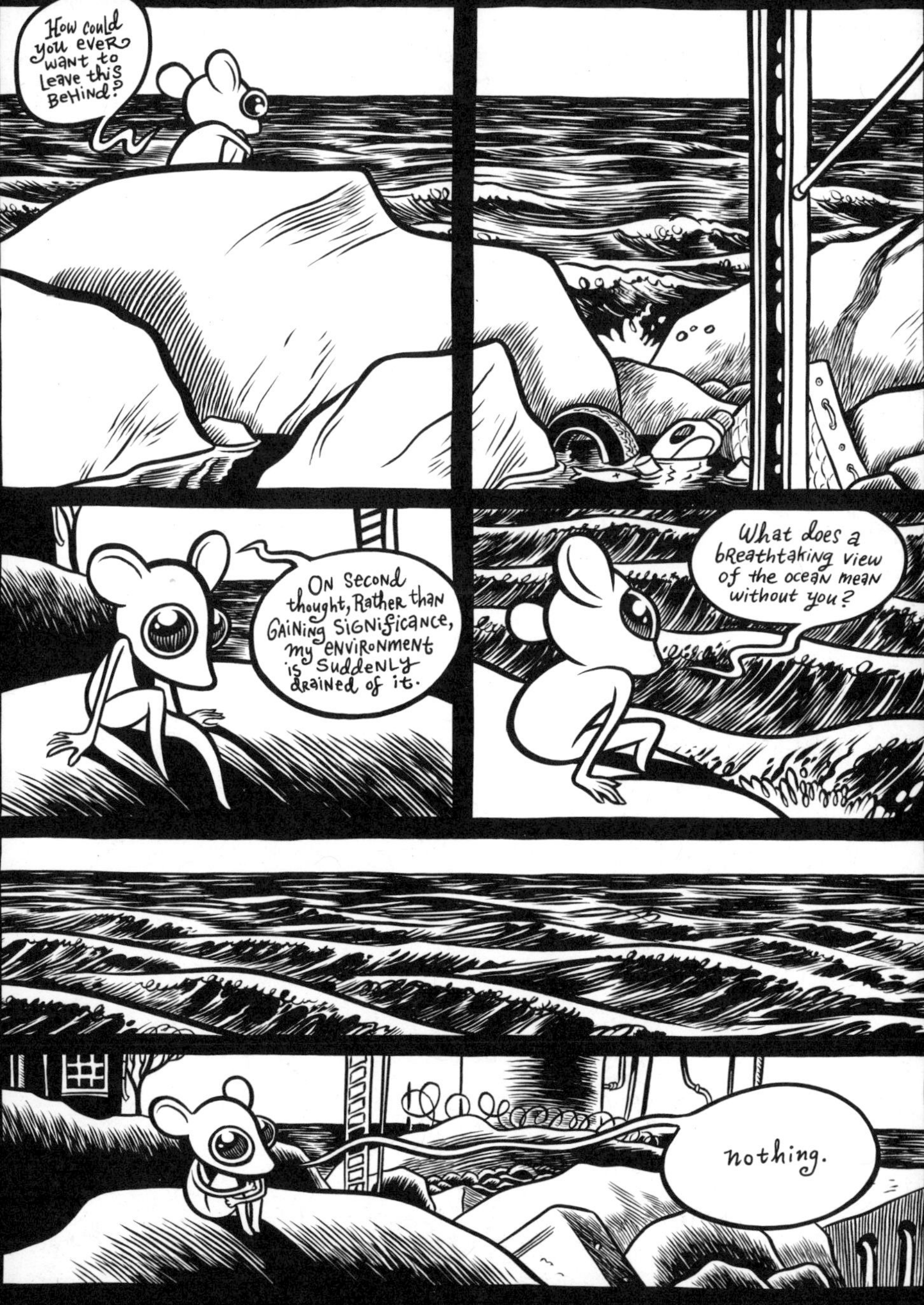
How could you ever want to leave this behind?
On second thought, rather than gaining significance, my environment is suddenly drained of it.
What does a breathtaking view of the ocean mean without you?
nothing.

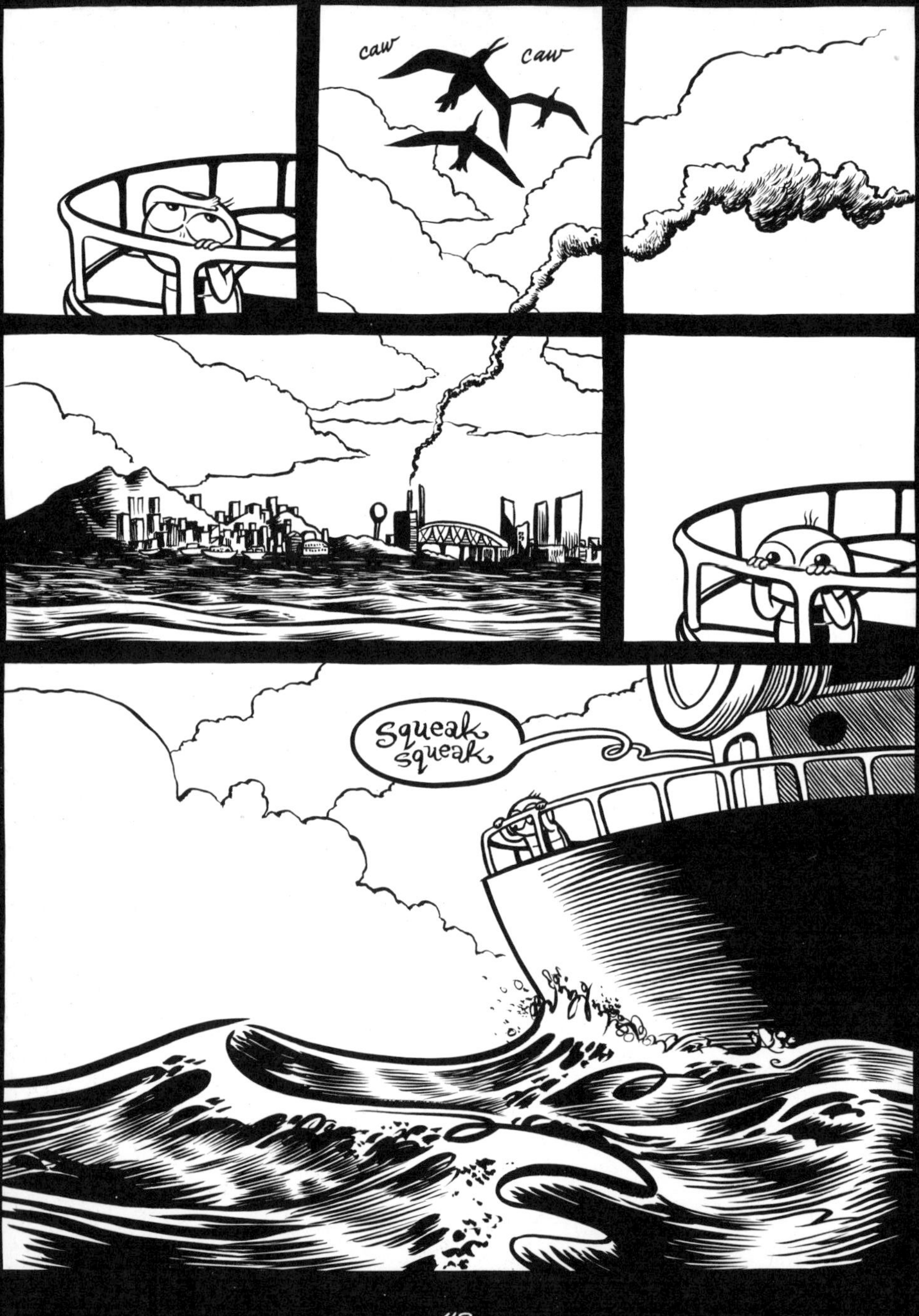
caw
caw
squeak squeak

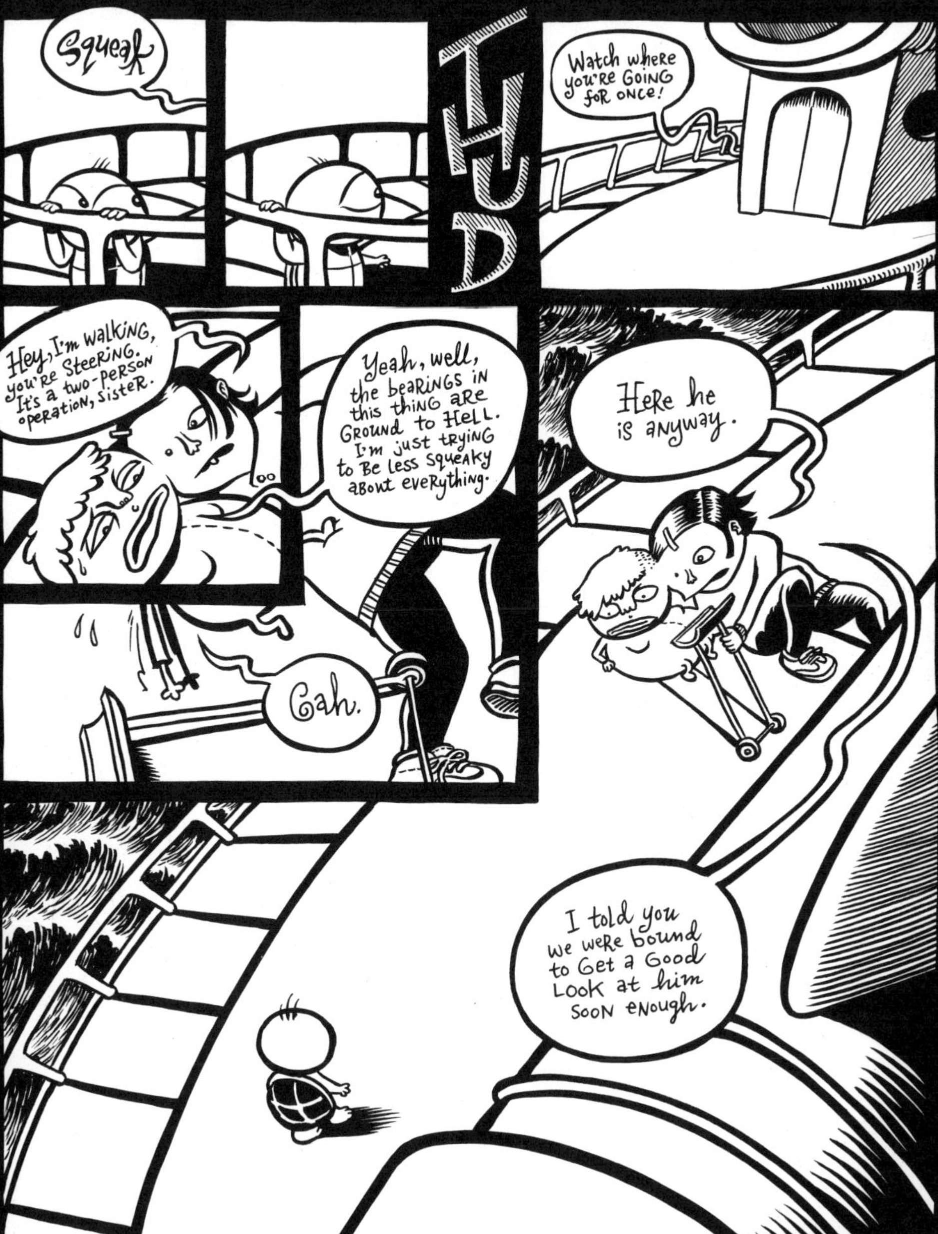
Squeak
THUD
Watch where you're GOING for once!
Hey, I'm walking, you're Steering. It's a two-person operation, sister.
Yeah, well, the bearings in this thing are Ground to Hell. I'm just trying to Be less squeaky about everything.
Gah.
Here he is anyway.
I told you we were bound to Get a Good Look at him soon enough.

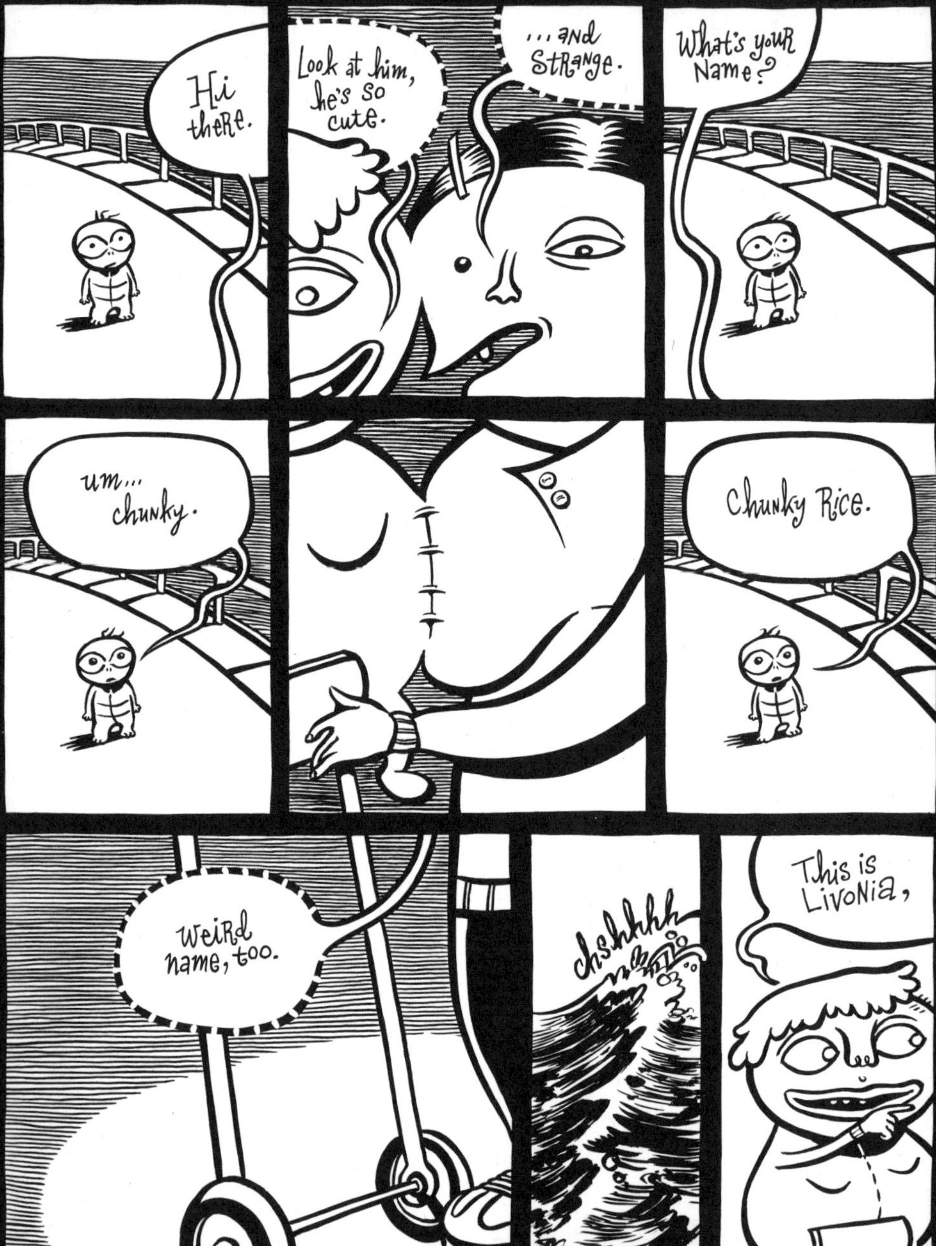
Hi there.
Look at him, he's so cute.
...and strange.
What's your Name?
um... chunky.
Chunky Rice.
weird name, too.
chshhhhh
This is Livonia,

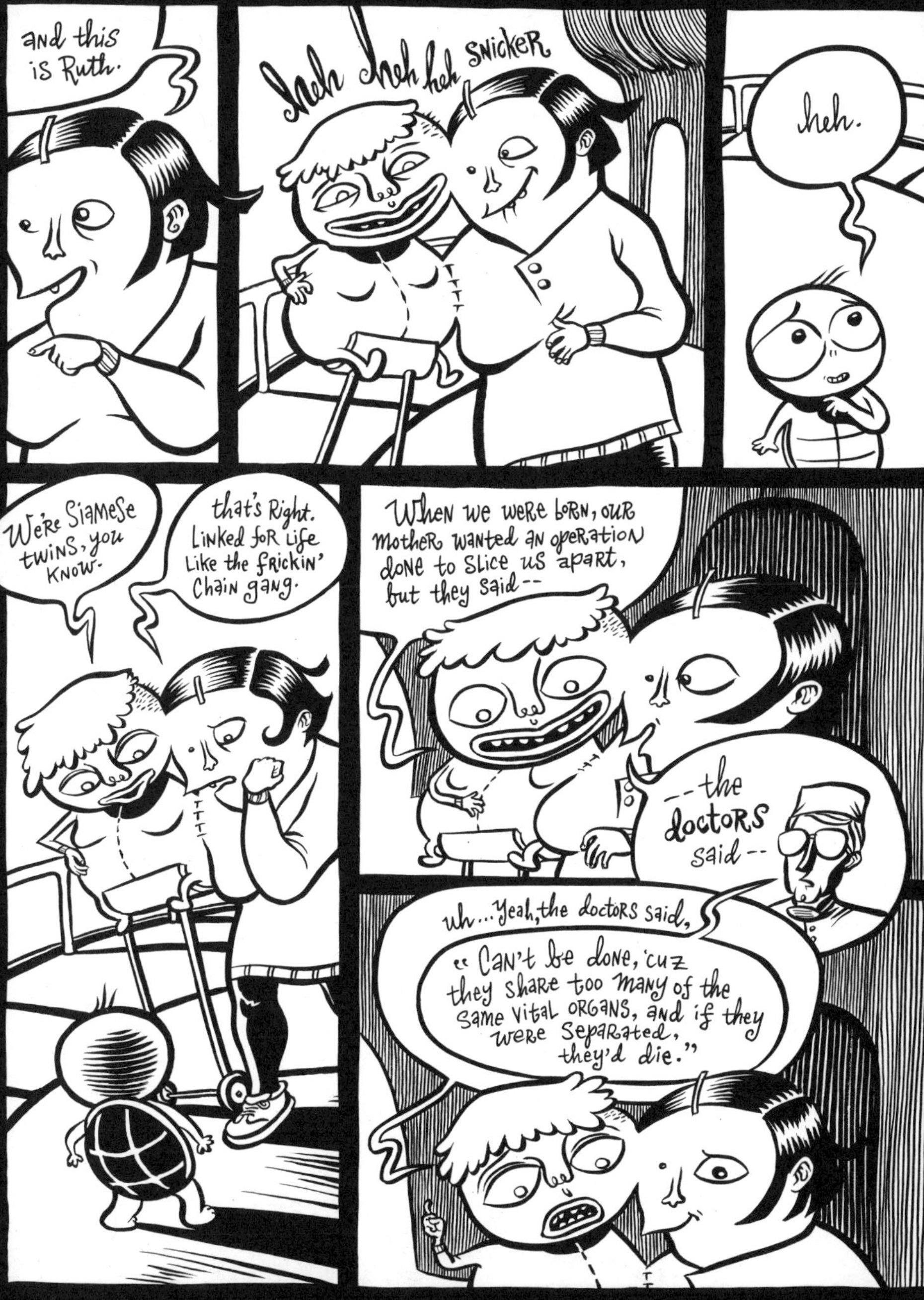
and this is Ruth.
heh heh heh SNICKER
heh.
We're Siamese twins, you know.
that's Right. Linked for life like the frickin' chain gang.
When we were born, our mother wanted an operation done to slice us apart, but they said--
--the doctors said--
uh...yeah, the doctors said,
"Can't be done, 'cuz they share too many of the same vital organs, and if they were separated, they'd die."

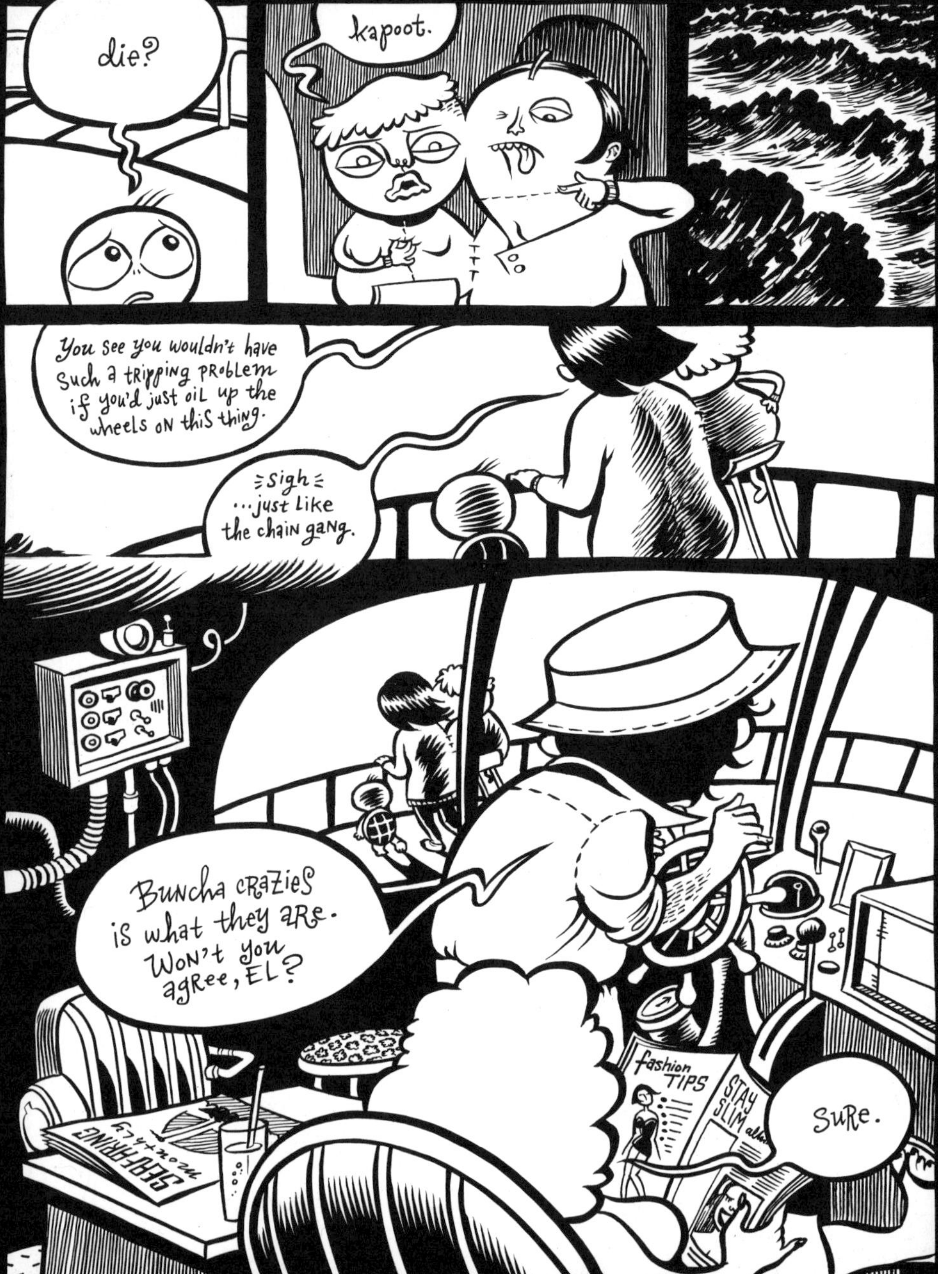
die?
kapoot.
You see you wouldn't have such a tripping problem if you'd just oil up the wheels on this thing.
sigh ...just like the chain gang.
Buncha crazies is what they are. Won't you agree, EL?
Sure.
fashion TIPS
STAY SLIM
SEAFARING monthly

53

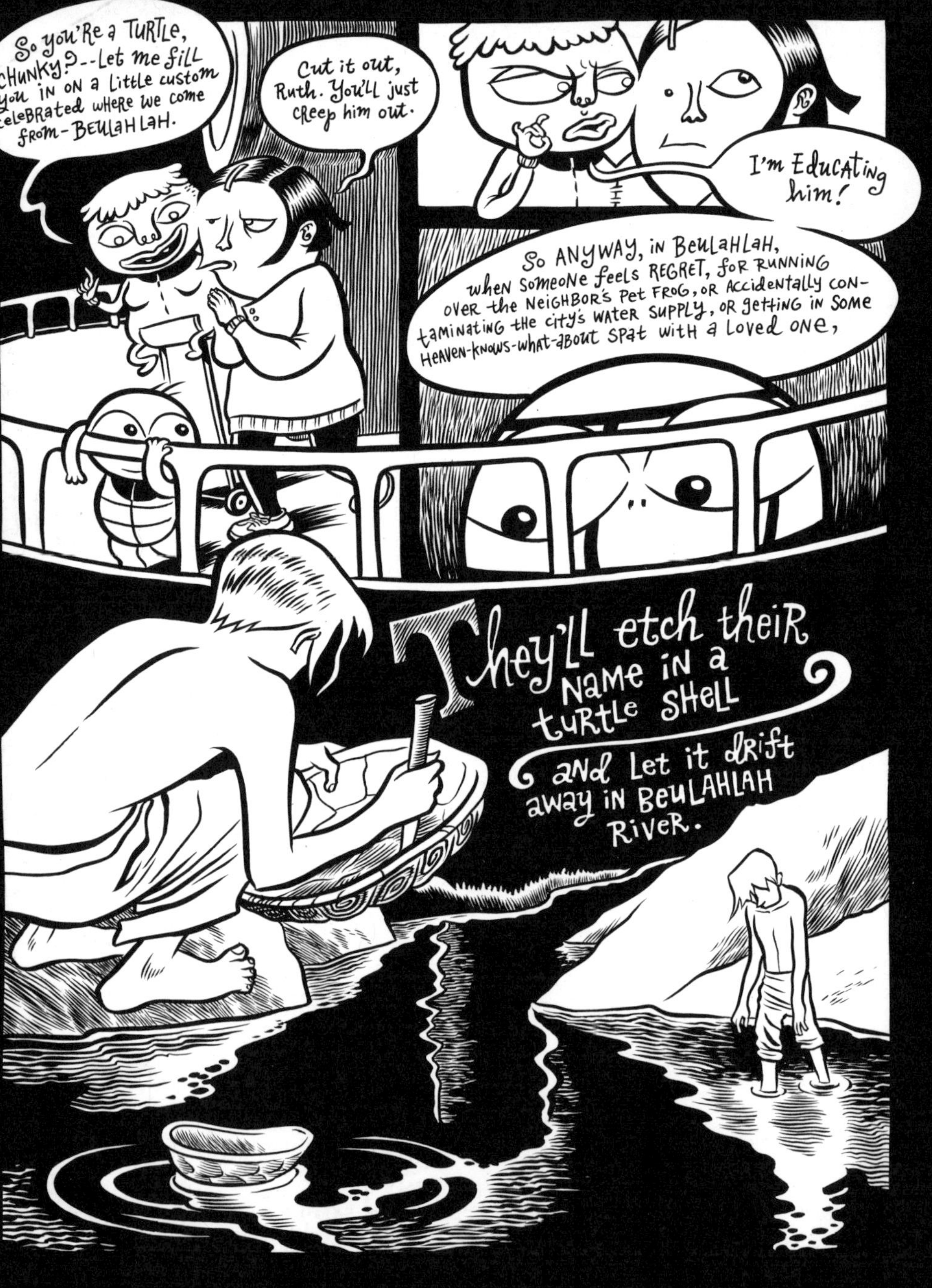

So you're a TURTLE, CHUNKY?--Let me fill you in on a little custom celebrated where we come from-BEULAHLAH.
Cut it out, Ruth. You'll just creep him out.
I'm Educating him!
So ANYWAY, in BEULAHLAH, when someone feels REGRET, for RUNNING over the NEIGHBOR'S Pet FROG, OR ACCIDENTALLY CON-TAMINATING the city's WATER SUPPLY, OR getting in some HEAVEN-KNOWS-WHAT-ABOUT SPAT WITH a Loved ONE,
They'll etch their NAME IN a turtle SHELL
and let it drift away in BEULAHLAH River.

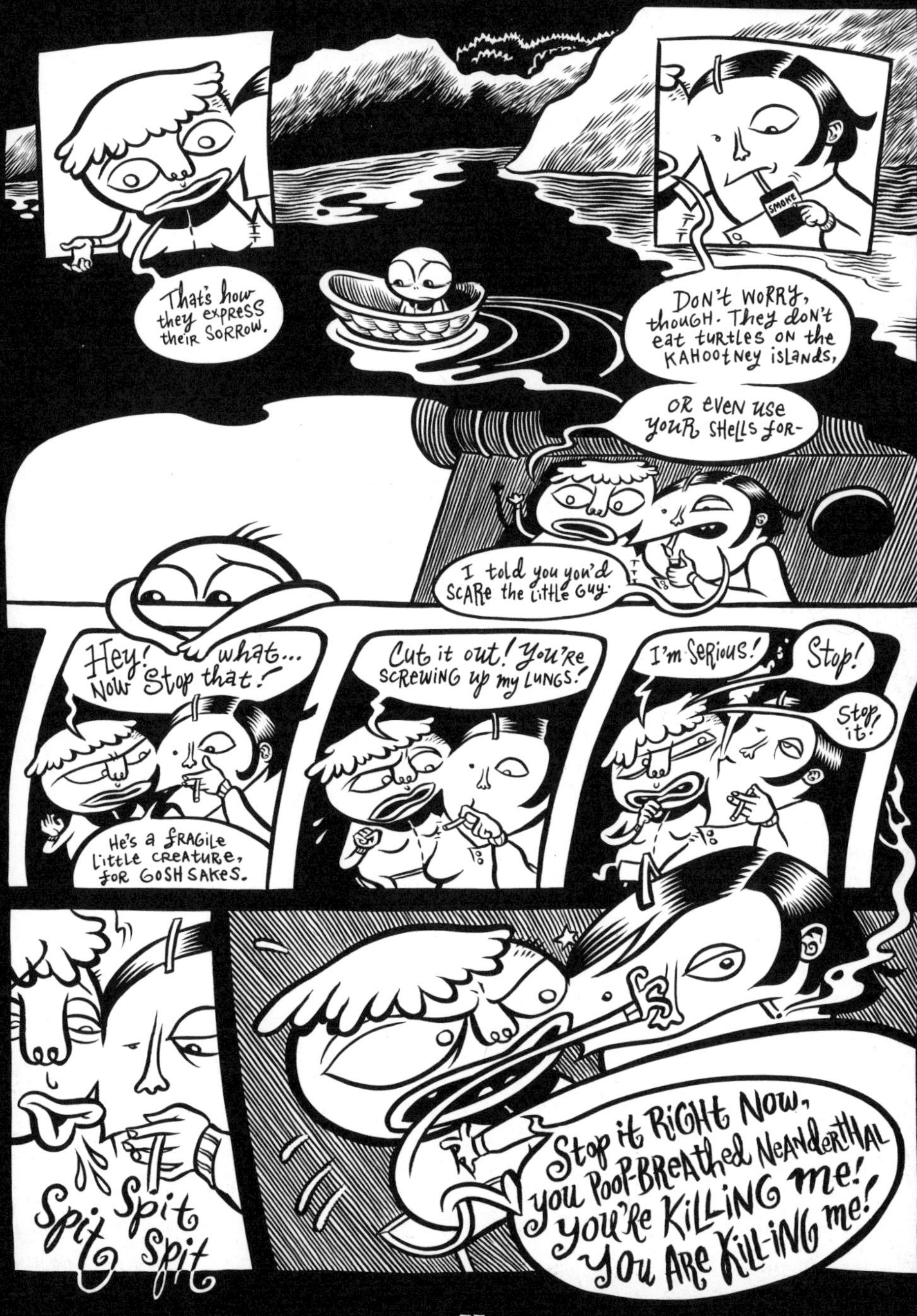
That's how they express their SORROW.
SMOKE
DON'T WORRY, though. They don't eat turtles on the KAHOOTNEY islands,
OR even use your shells for-
I told you you'd SCARE the little Guy.
Hey! what... Now Stop that!
He's a FRAGILE little creature, for GOSH SAKES.
Cut it out! You're SCREWING up my LUNGS!
I'm Serious!
Stop!
Stop it!
Spit Spit Spit Spit
Stop it RIGHT NOW, you Poop-BREAThed NEANDERTHAL you're KILLING me! You ARE KILL-ING me!

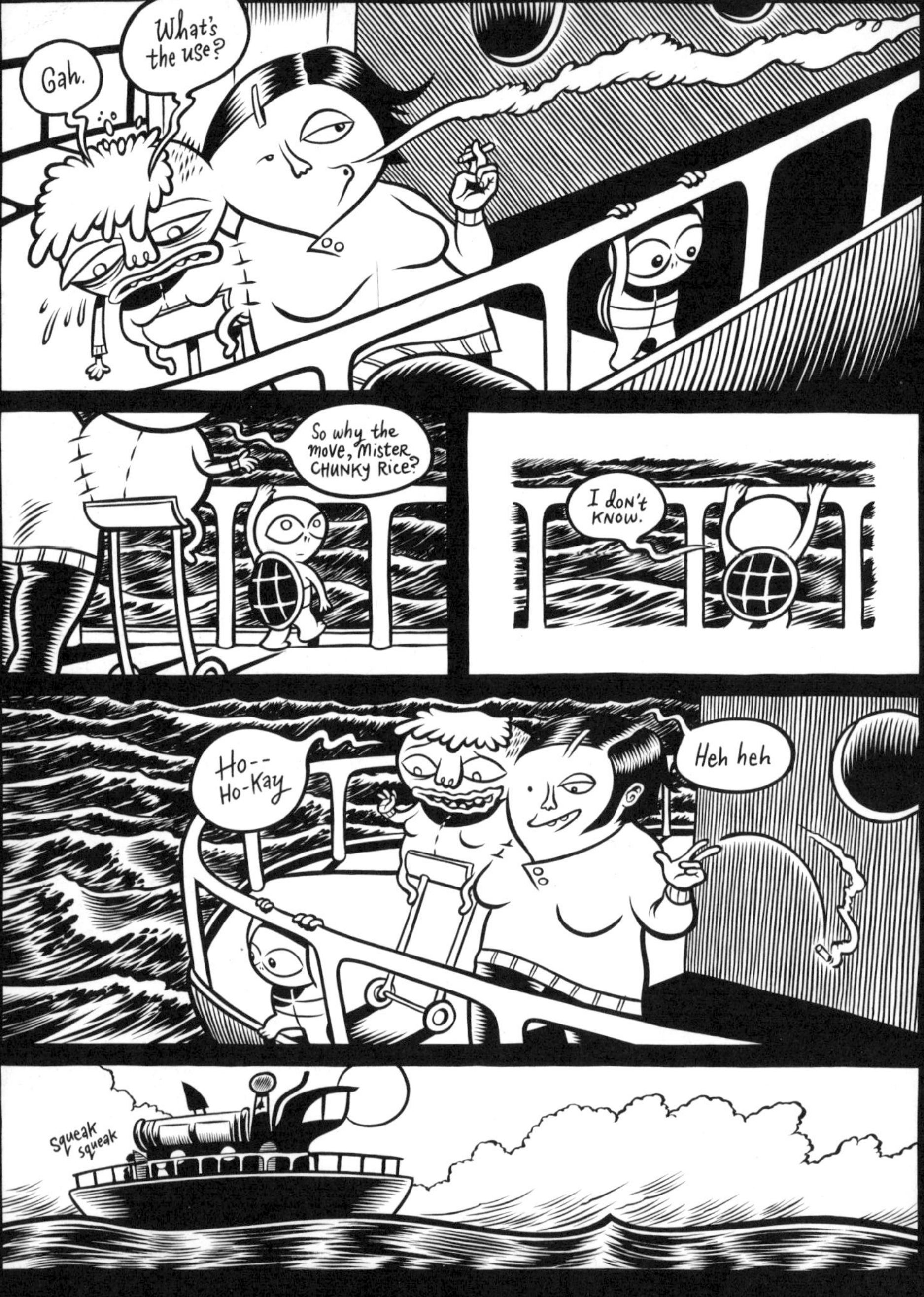
Gah.
What's the use?
So why the move, Mister CHUNKY Rice?
I don't know.
Ho--
Ho-Kay
Heh heh
squeak squeak

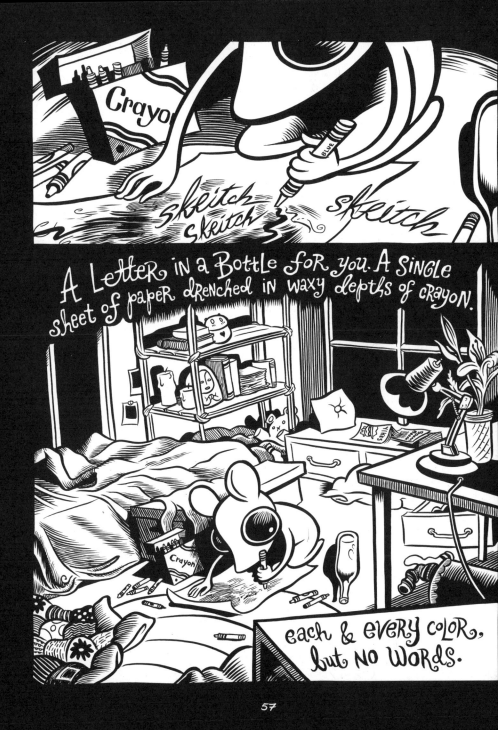

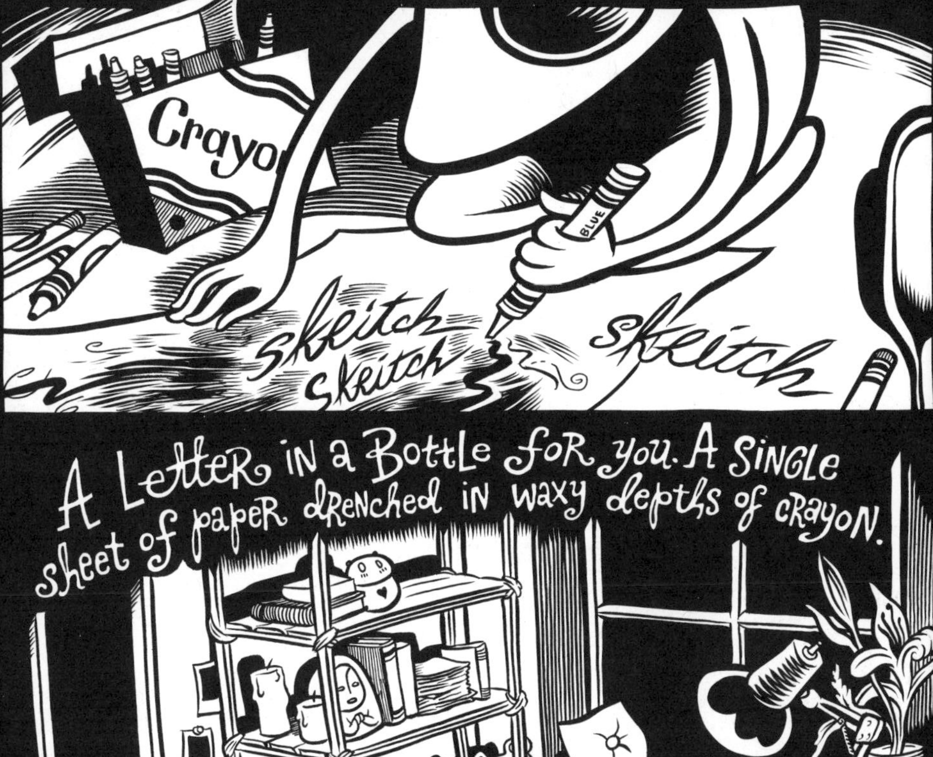
Crayo
BLUE
skritch
skritch
skritch
A letter in a bottle for you. A single sheet of paper drenched in waxy depths of crayon.
YIKES
Crayon
each & every color, but no words.

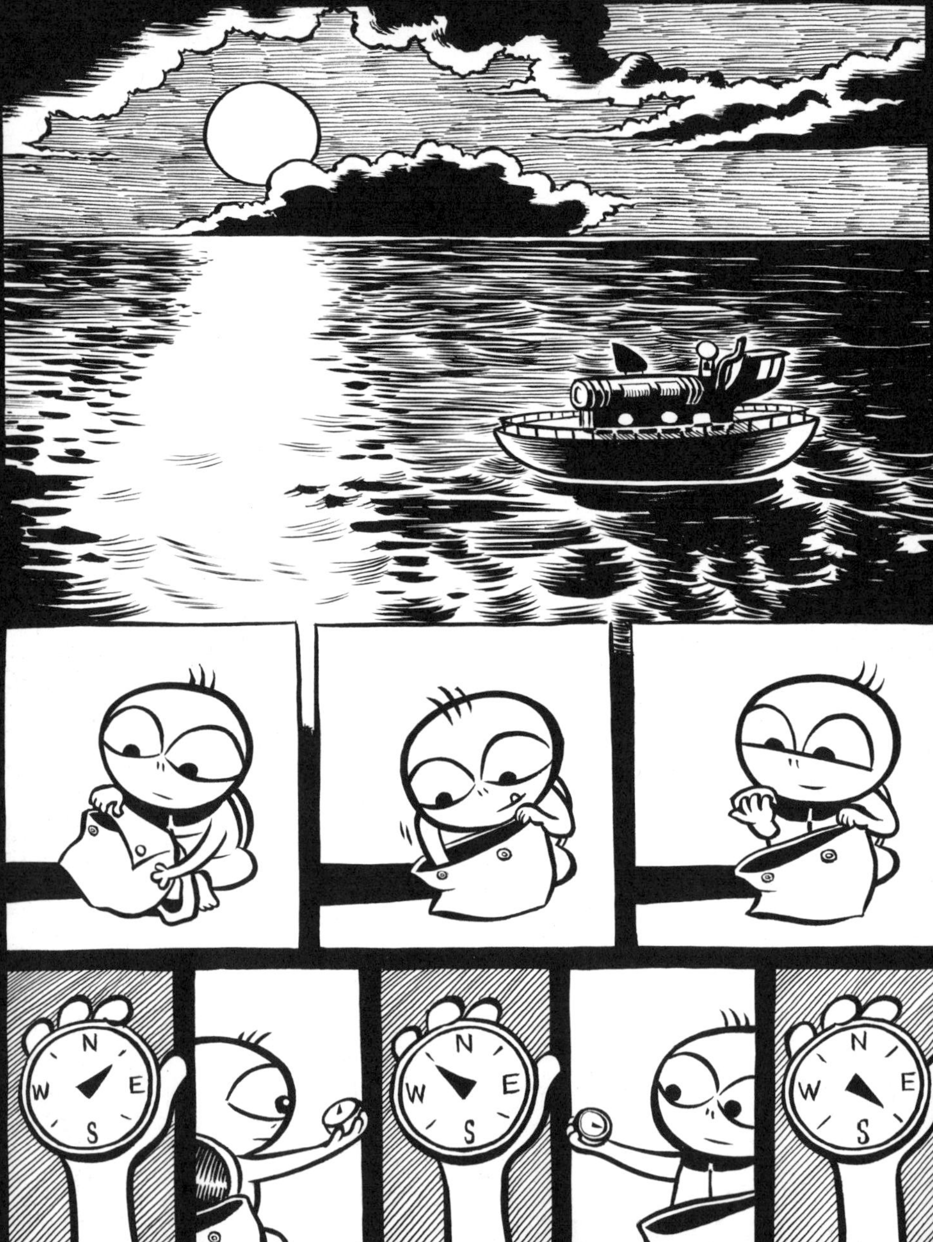
N
W
E
S
N
W
E
S
N
W
E
S

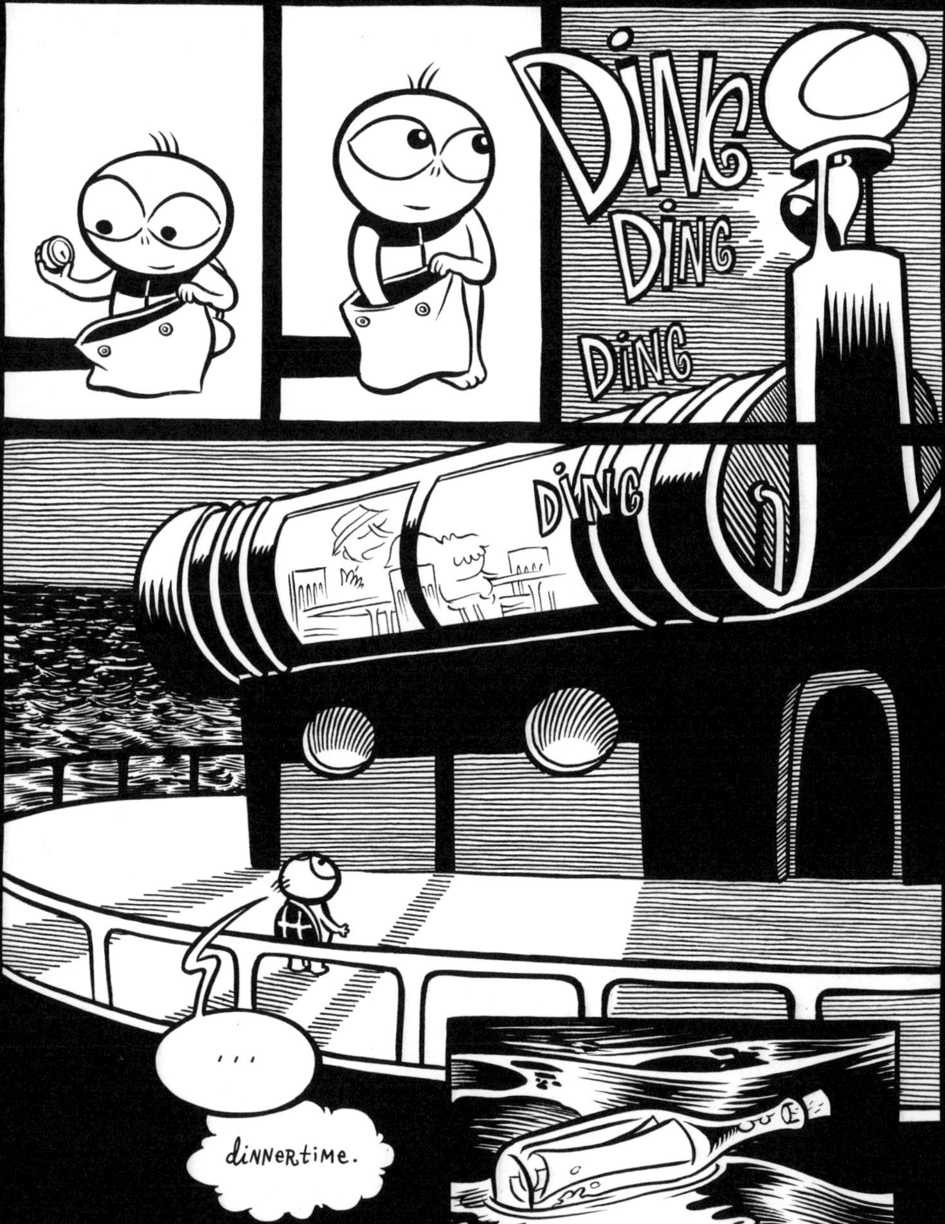
DING
DING
DING
DING
...
dinnertime.

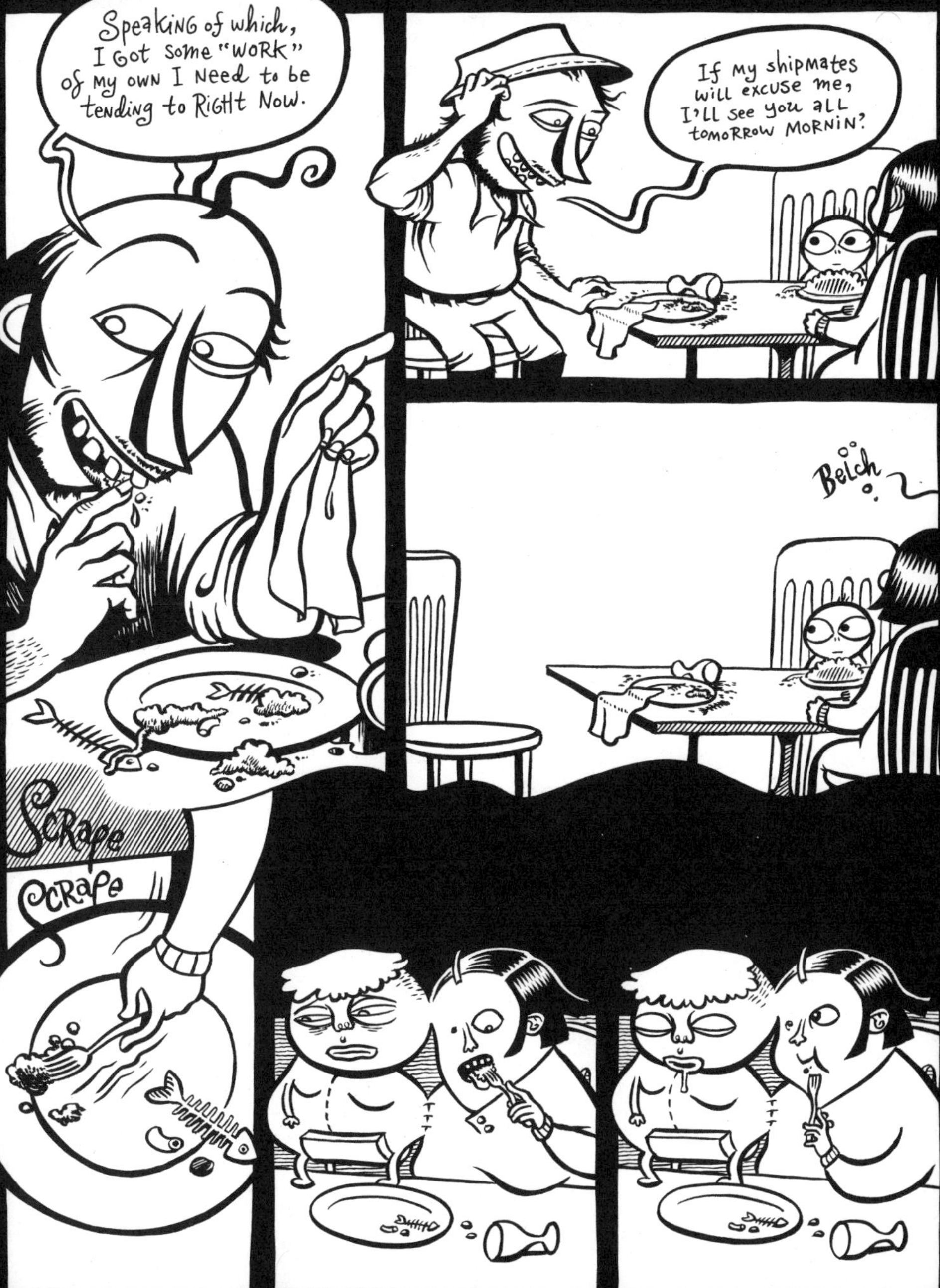
Speaking of which, I got some "WORK" of my own I need to be tending to RIGHT NOW.
If my shipmates will excuse me, I'll see you all tomorrow mornin'.
Belch
Scrape
Scrape

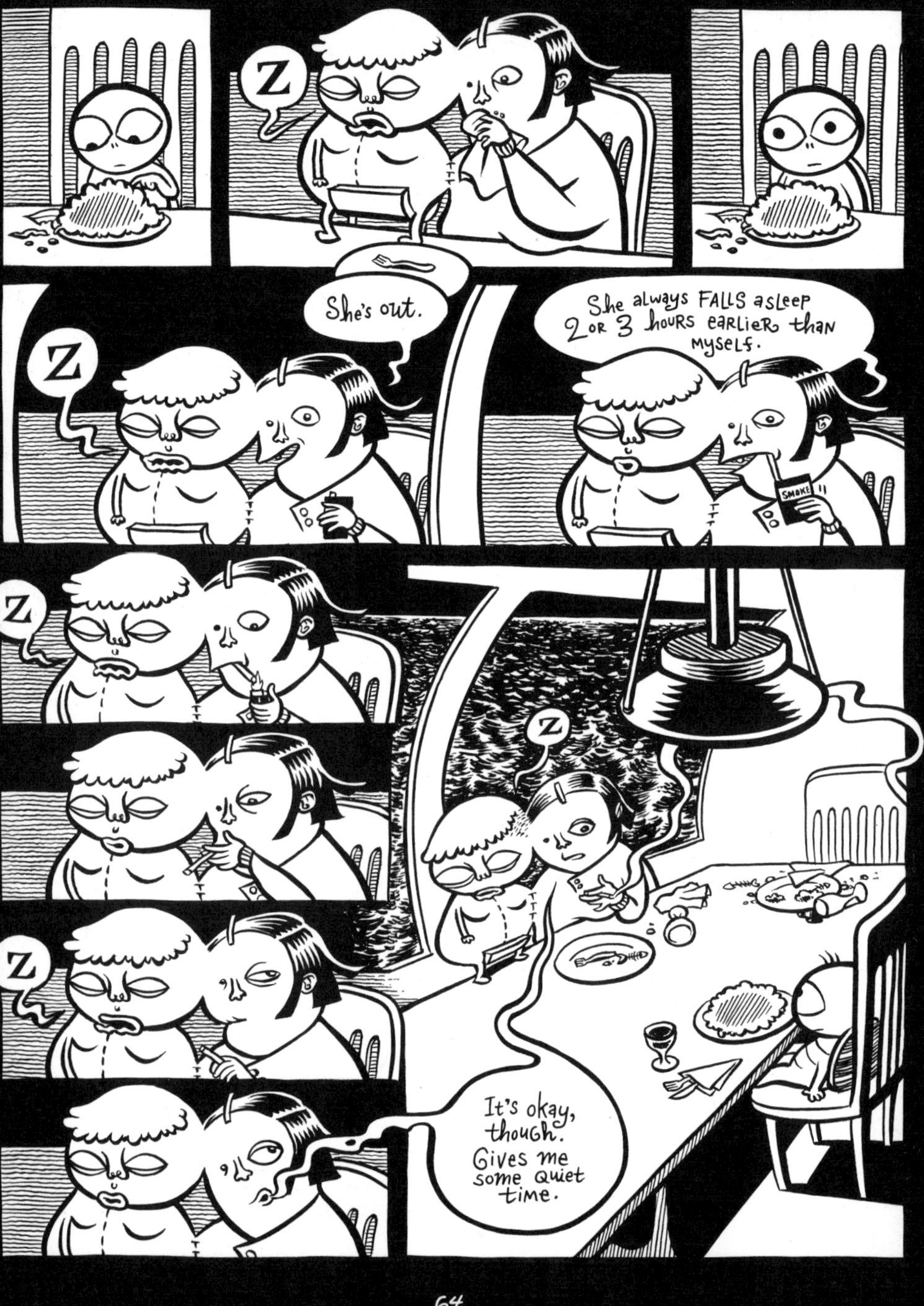

Z
Z
She's out.
She always FALLS asleep 2 or 3 hours earlier than myself.
SMOKE
Z
Z
Z
It's okay, though. Gives me some quiet time.

65

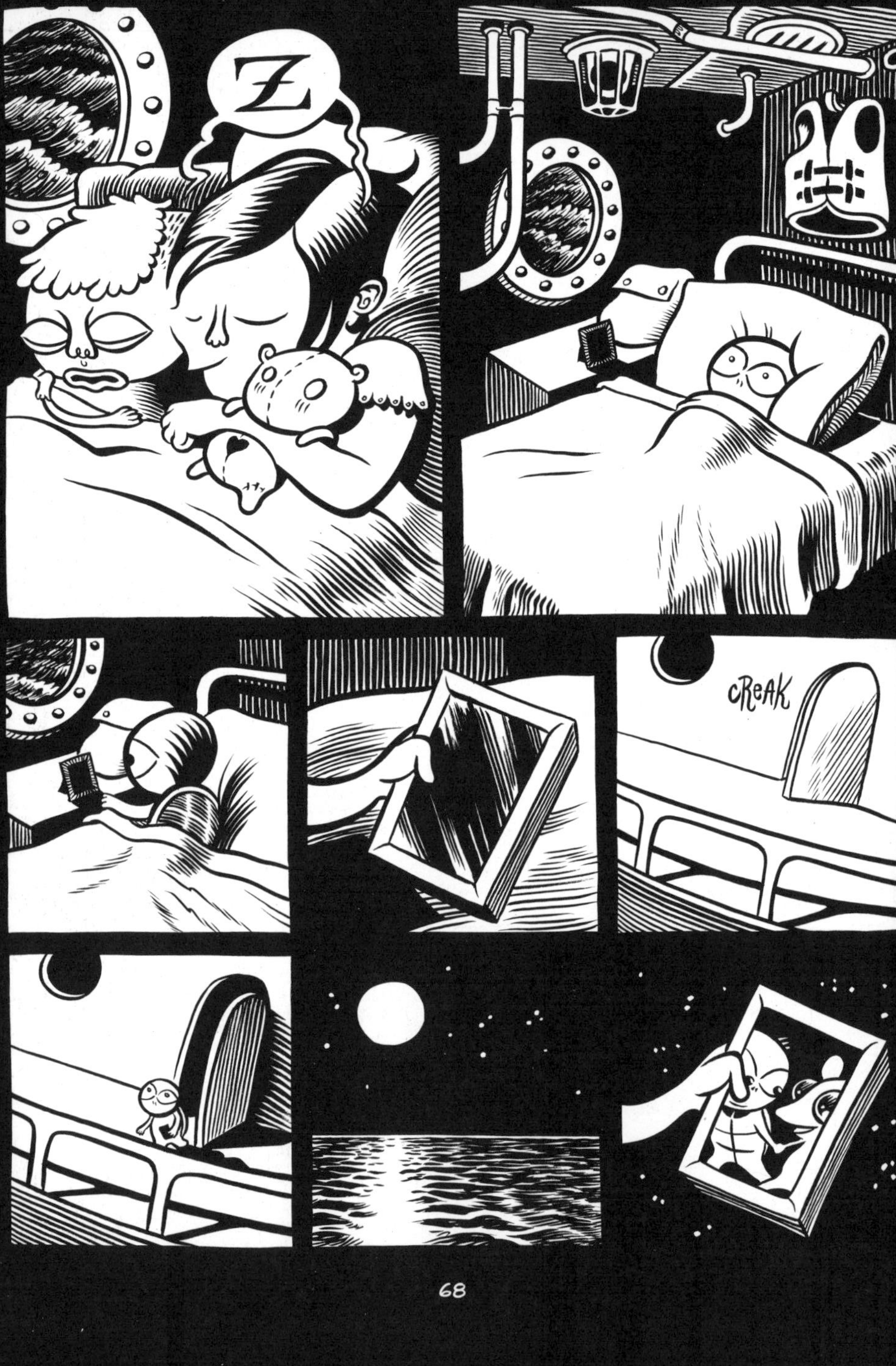
Z
CREAK

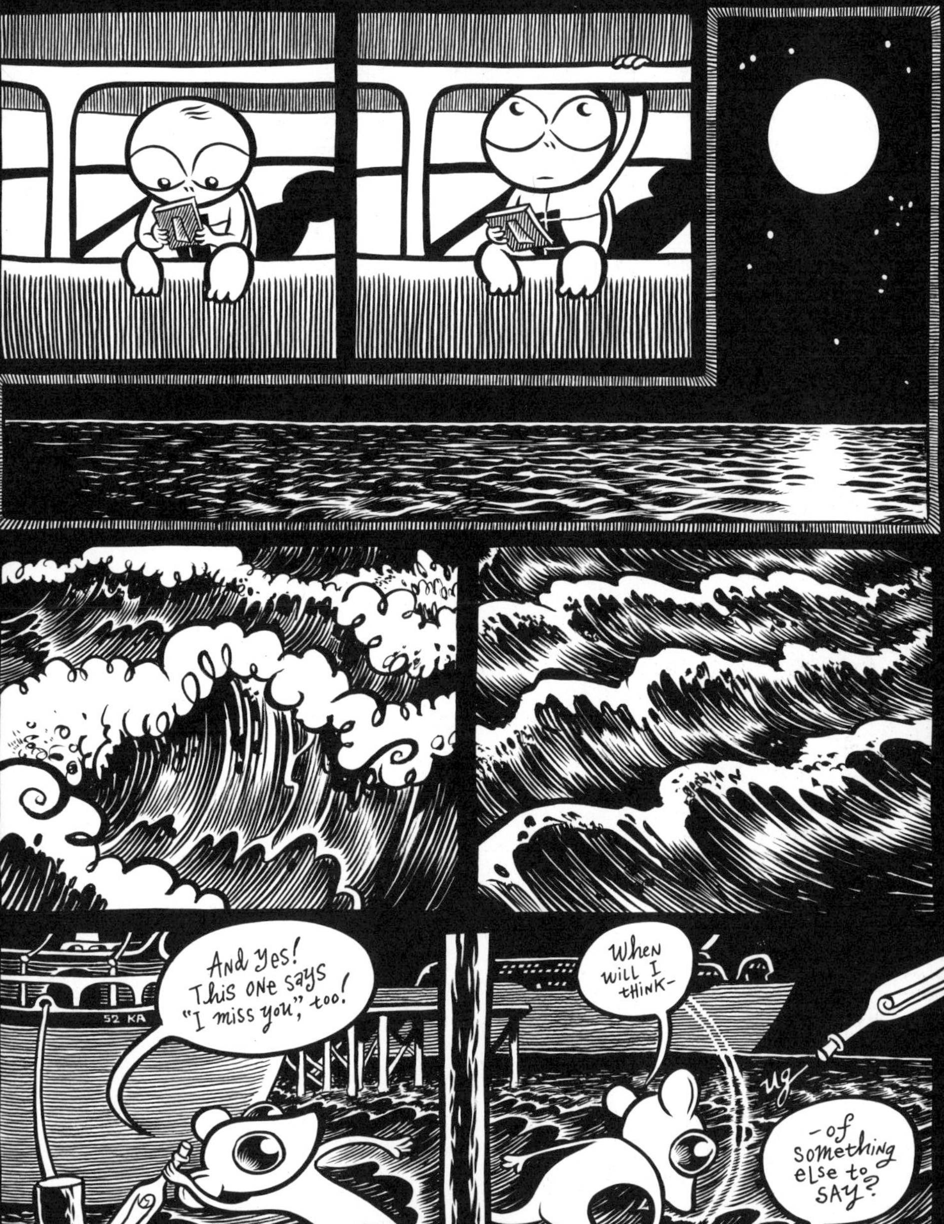
52 KA
And yes! This one says "I miss you," too!
When will I think-
ug
-of something else to SAY?

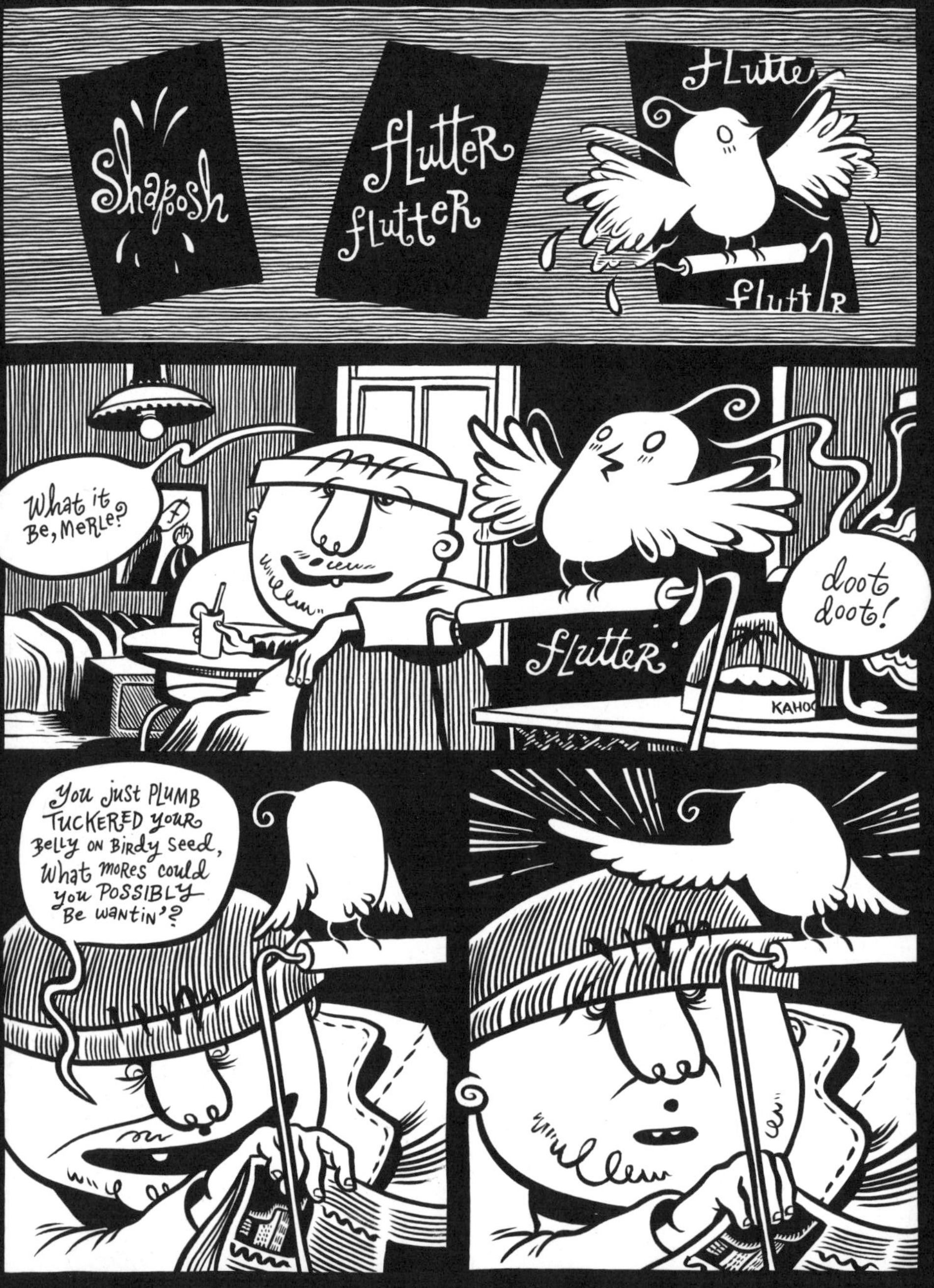
Shaposh
flutter
flutter
flutte
flutt R
What it Be, Merle?
flutter
doot doot!
KAHO
You just PLUMB TUCKERED your Belly on Birdy seed, What mores could you POSSIBLY Be wantin'?

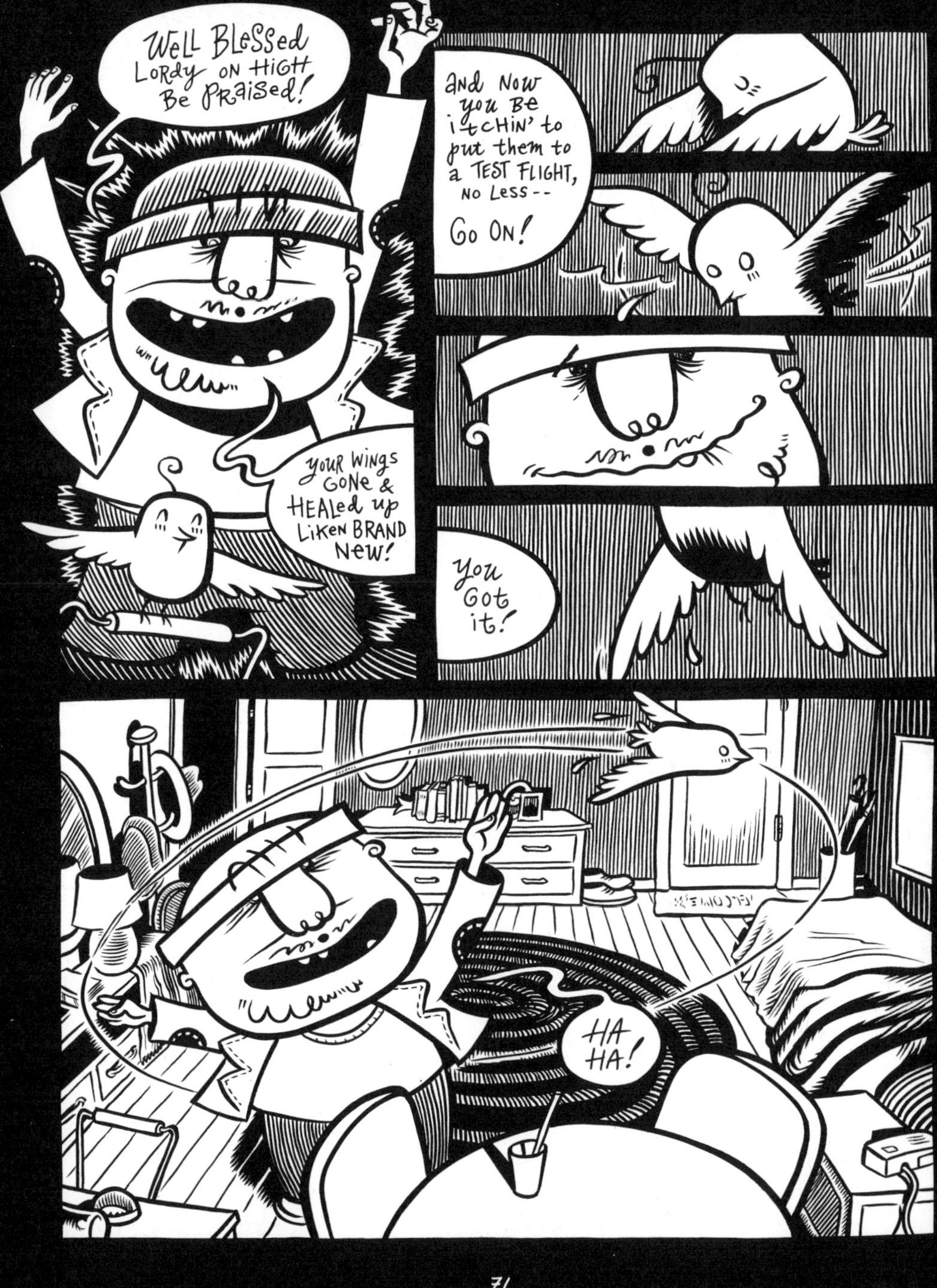
WELL BLESSED LORDY ON HIGH BE PRAISED!
YOUR WINGS GONE & HEALED UP LIKEN BRAND NEW!
AND NOW YOU BE ITCHIN' TO PUT THEM TO A TEST FLIGHT, NO LESS--
GO ON!
YOU GOT IT!
HA HA!

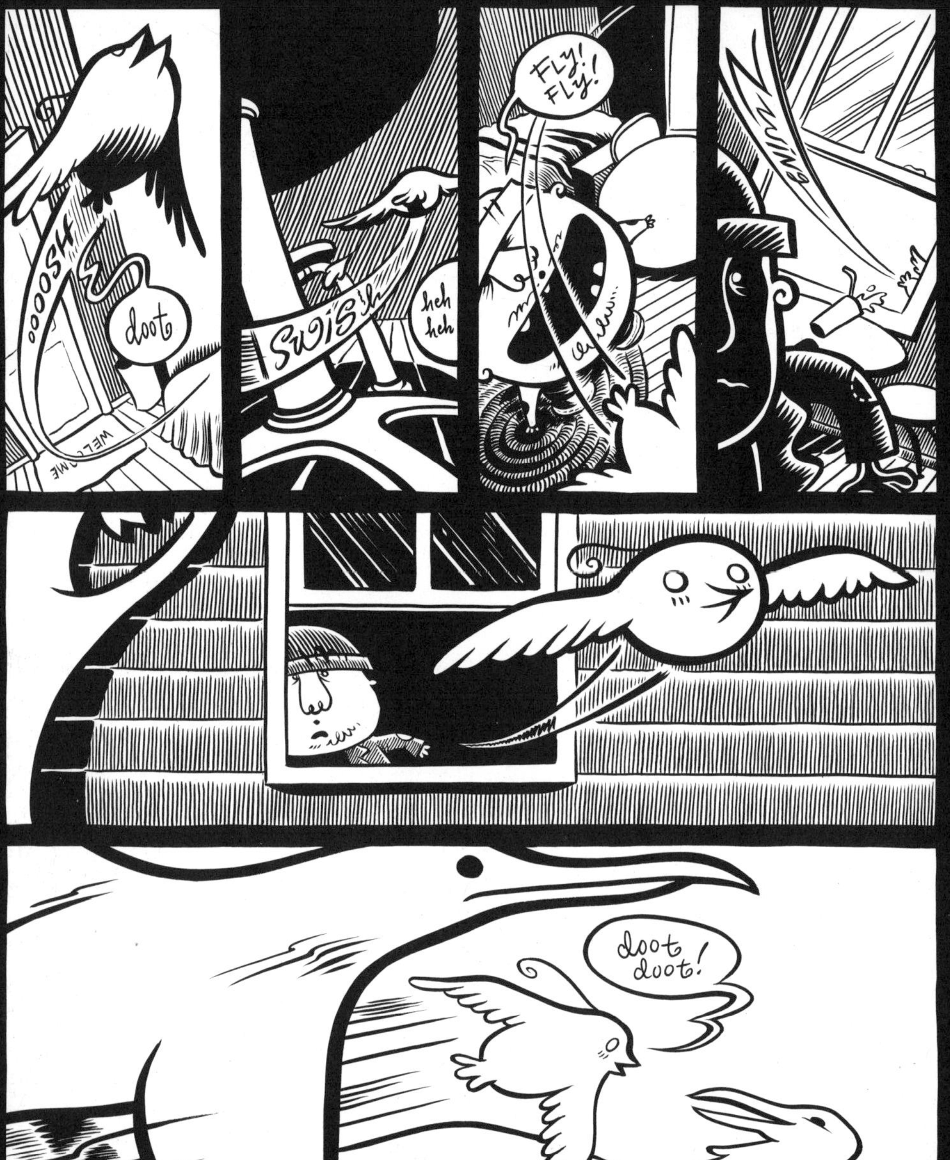
ooooSH
doot
WELCOME
SWISH
heh heh
FLY! FLY!
ZWING
doot doot!

MERLE! No! Come Back!
caw
caw
MERLE ...
MERLE ...
...

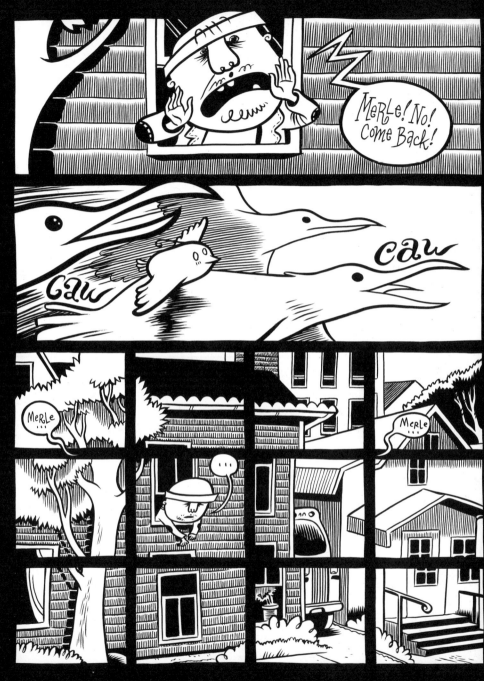

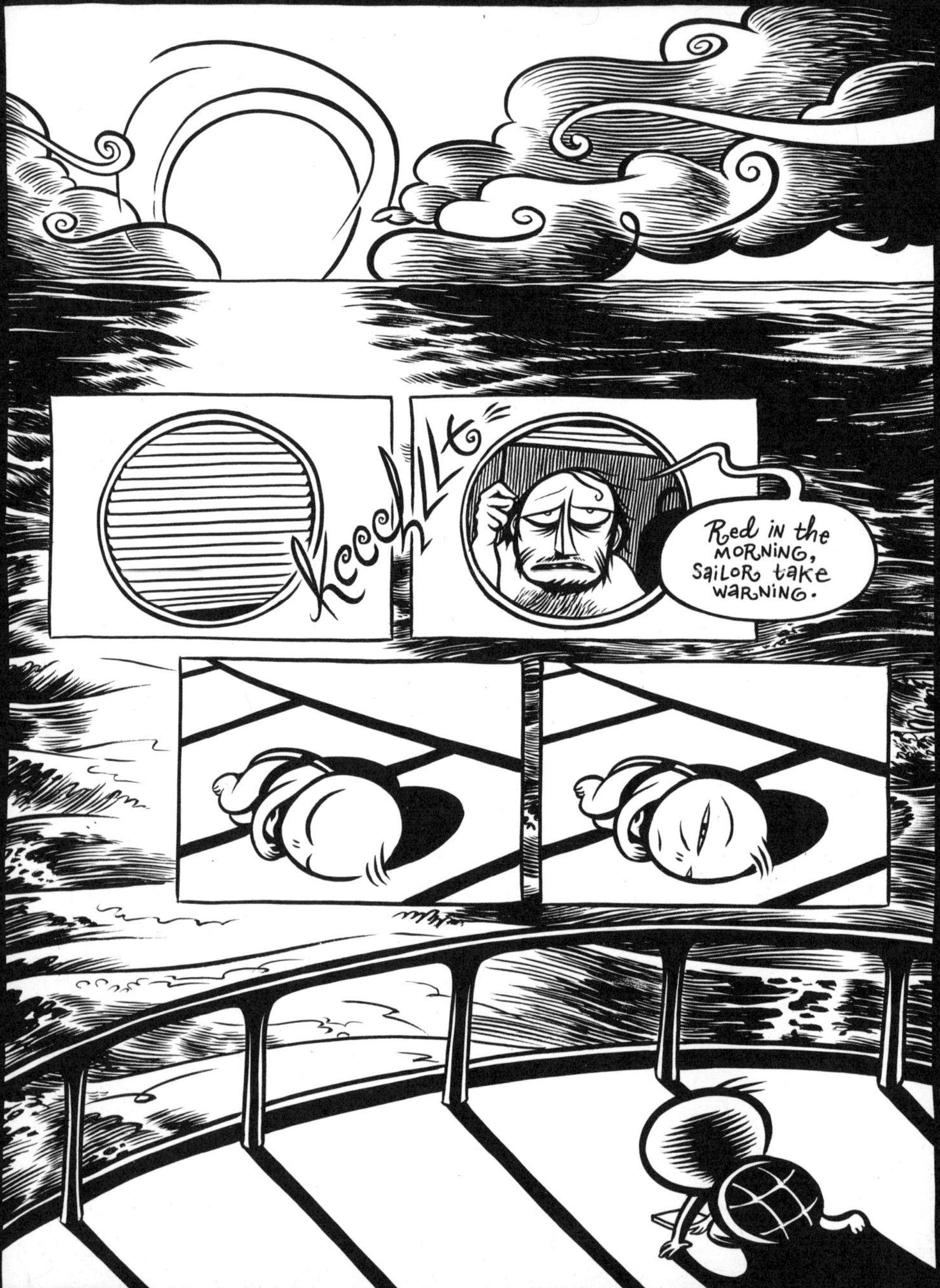
kccchllt
Red in the MORNING, Sailor take WARNING.

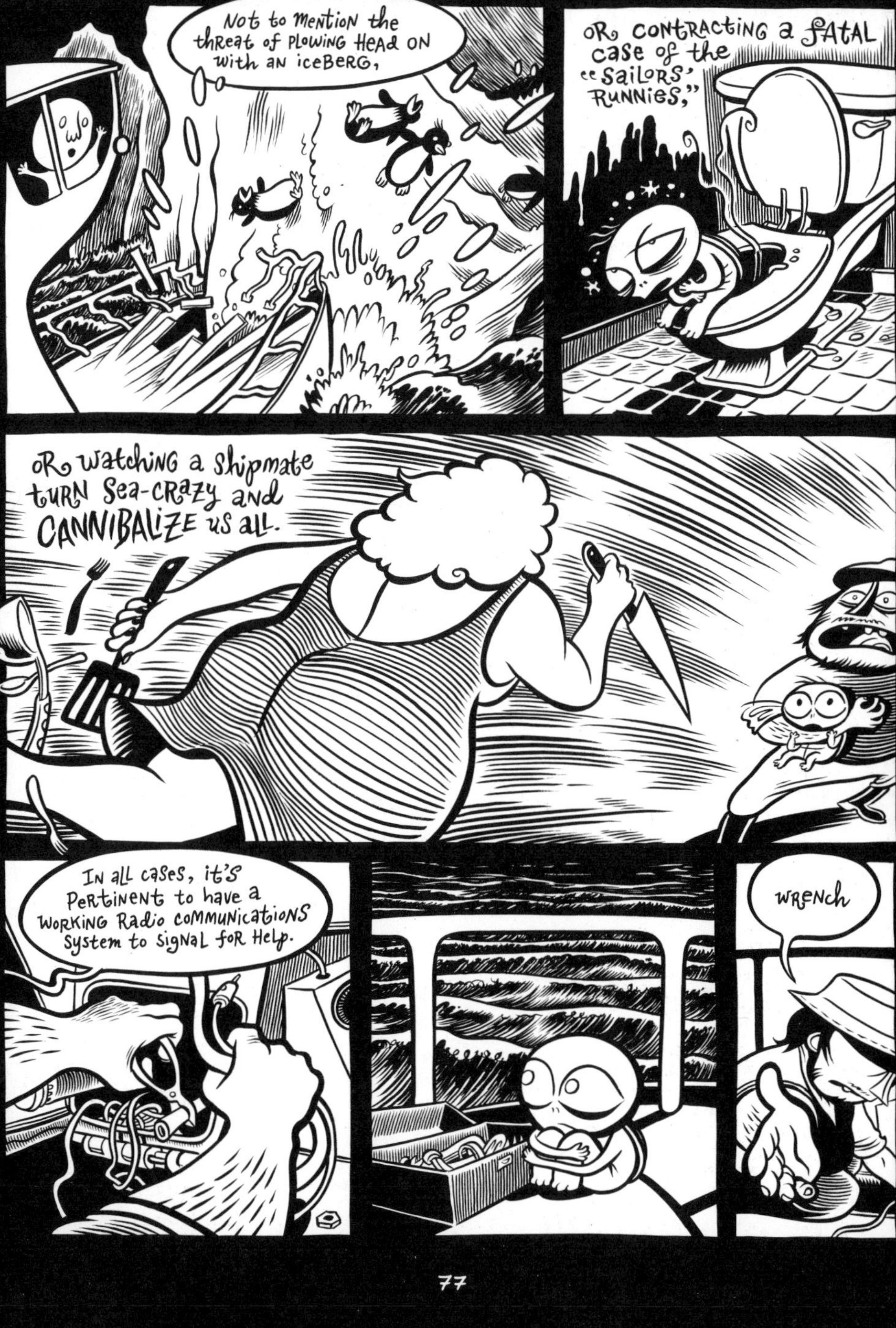
Not to mention the threat of plowing head on with an iceberg,
or contracting a fatal case of the "sailors' runnies,"
or watching a shipmate turn sea-crazy and cannibalize us all.
In all cases, it's pertinent to have a working radio communications system to signal for help.
wrench

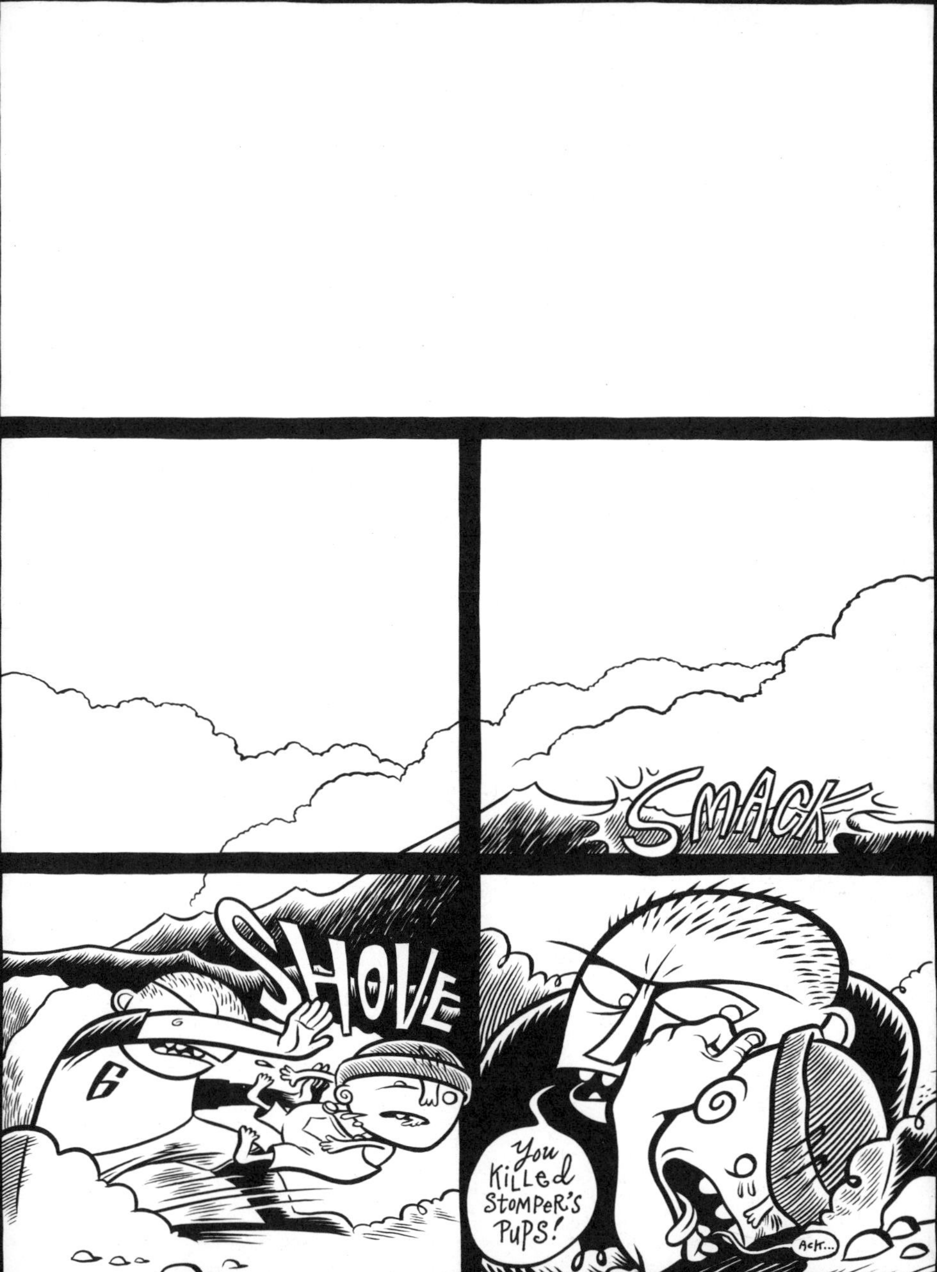
SMACK
SHOVE
You Killed Stomper's Pups!
Ack...

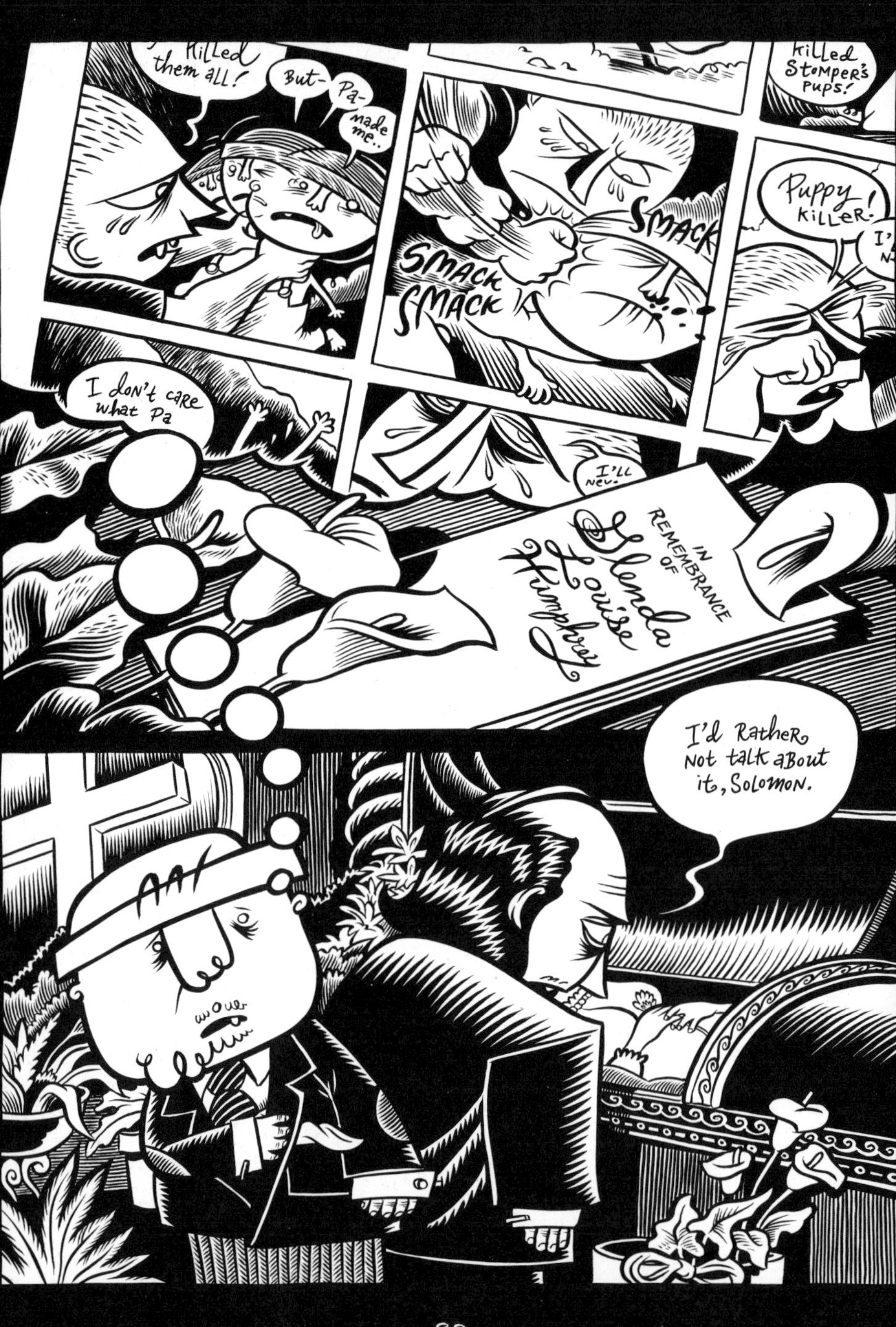

Killed them all!
But-
Pa-
made me..
Killed Stomper's pups!
SMACK
SMACK
SMACK
Puppy! KILLER-
I don't care what Pa
I'll nev-
IN REMEMBRANCE OF
Glenda Louise Humphrey
I'd Rather not talk about it, Solomon.

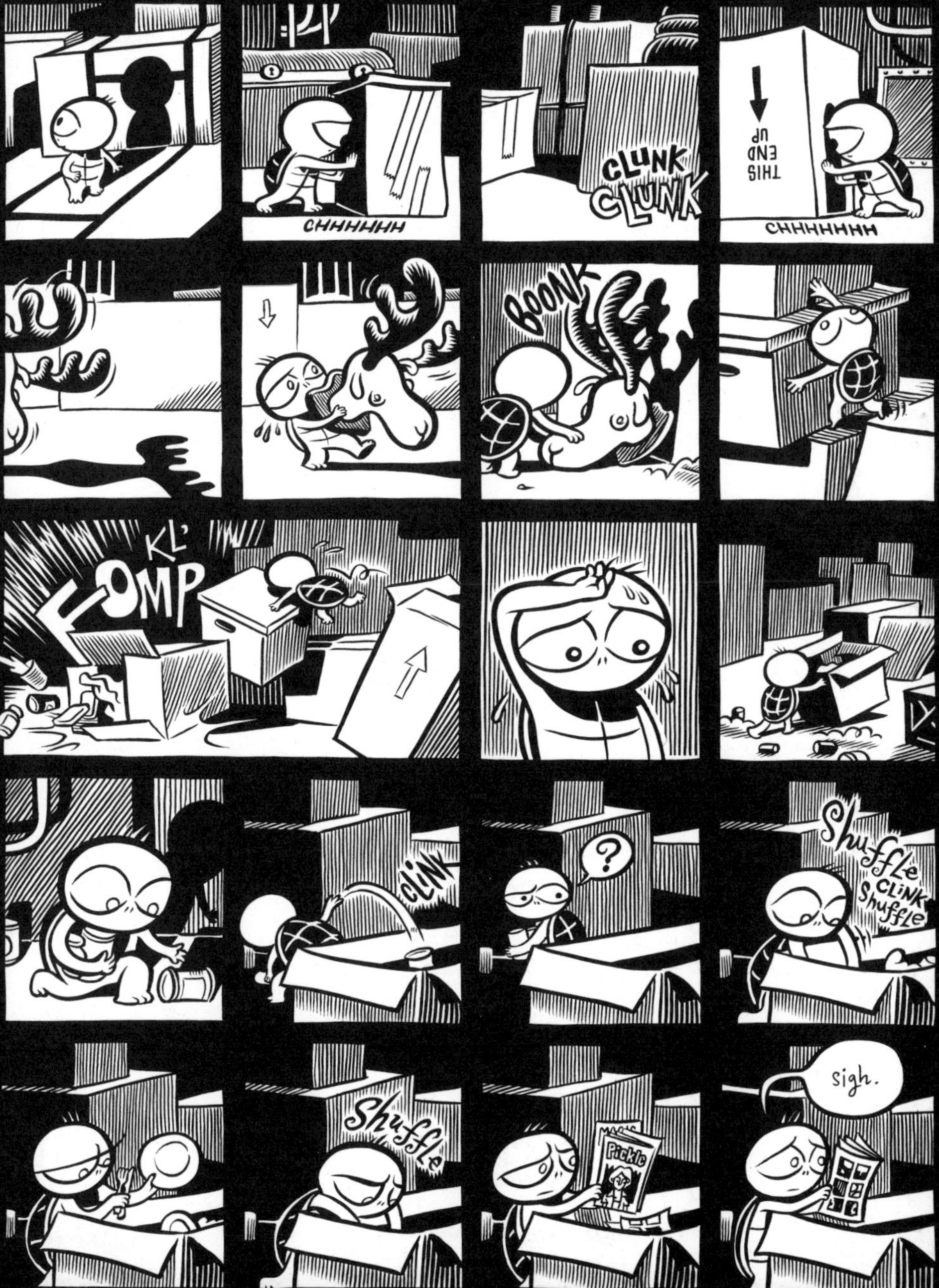
CHHHHHH
CLUNK
CLUNK
THIS END UP
CHHHHHHH
BOONK
KL' FOMP
CLINK
?
Shuffle
CLINK
Shuffle
Shuffle
Pickle
sigh.

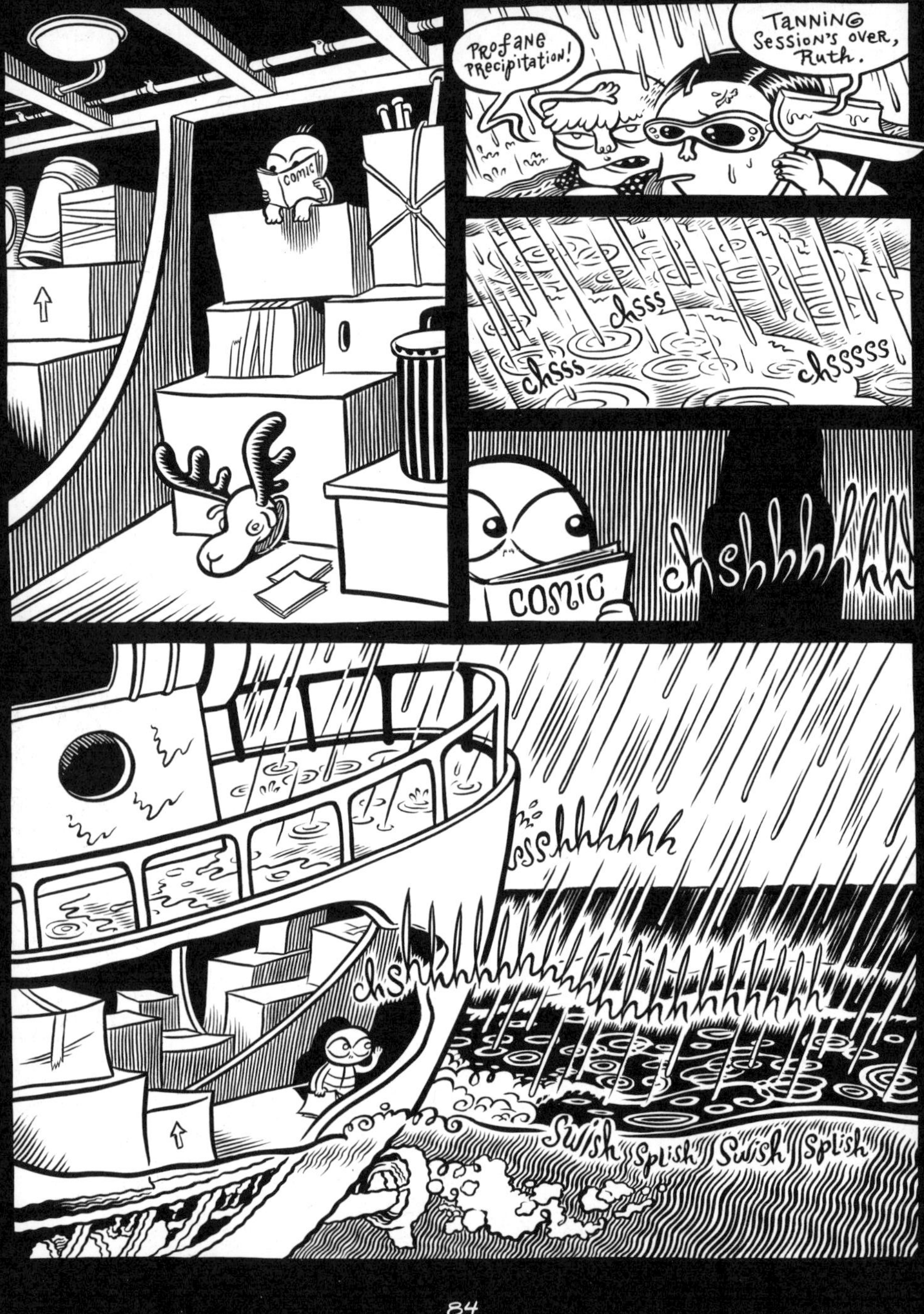

COMIC
Profane Precipitation!
Tanning Session's over, Ruth.
chsss
chsss
chsssss
COMIC
chshhhhhh
sshhhhhh
chshhhhhhhhhhhhhhhhhhhhh
Swish splish Swish splish

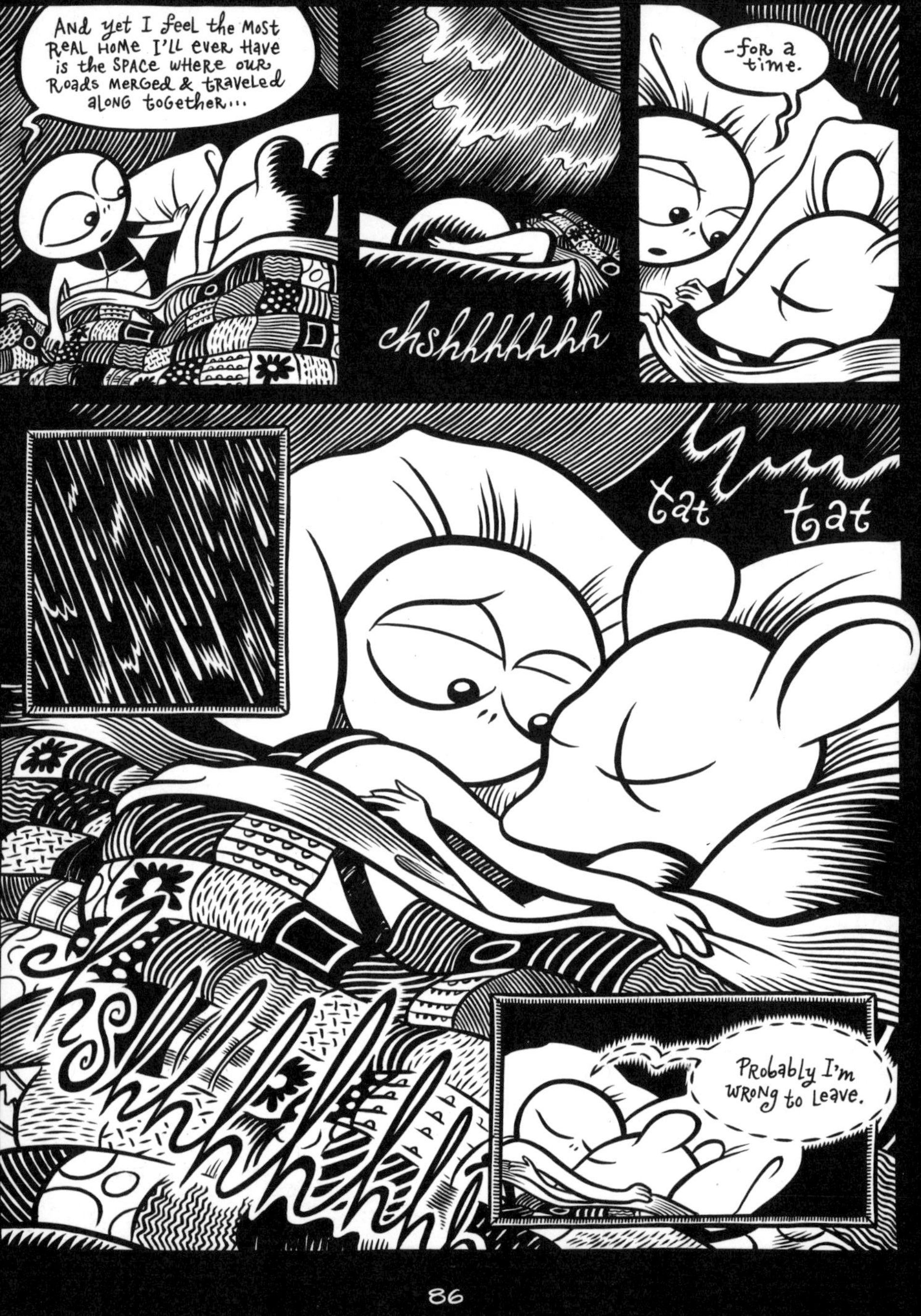
And yet I feel the most real home I'll ever have is the space where our roads merged & traveled along together...
chshhhhhhhh
-for a time.
tat tat
chshhhhhhhh
Probably I'm wrong to leave.

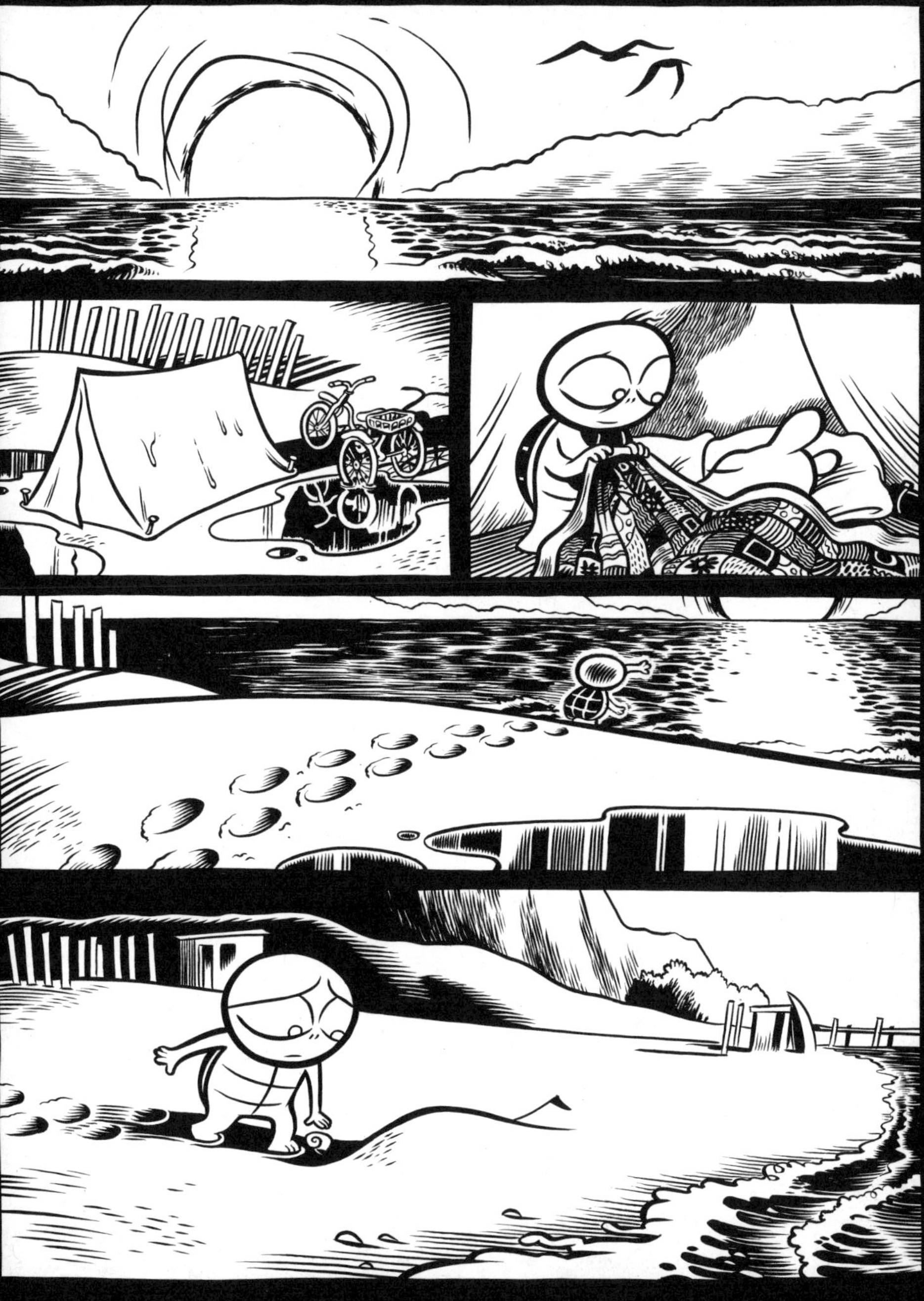

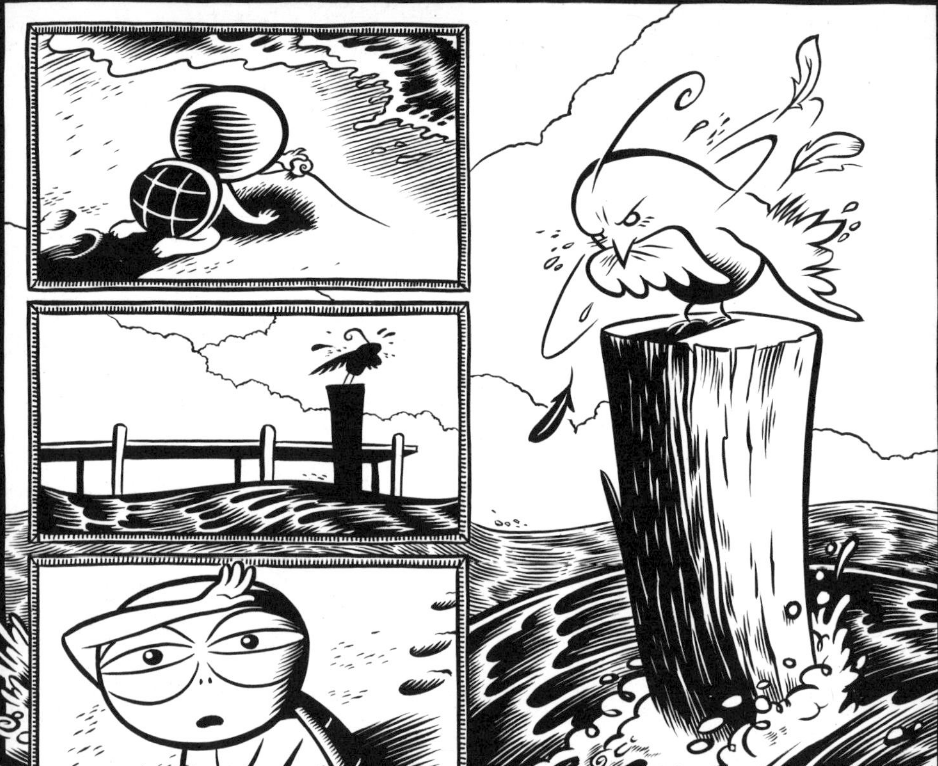
RiP
SHRed
TeAR
Hey, early bird, what's up?

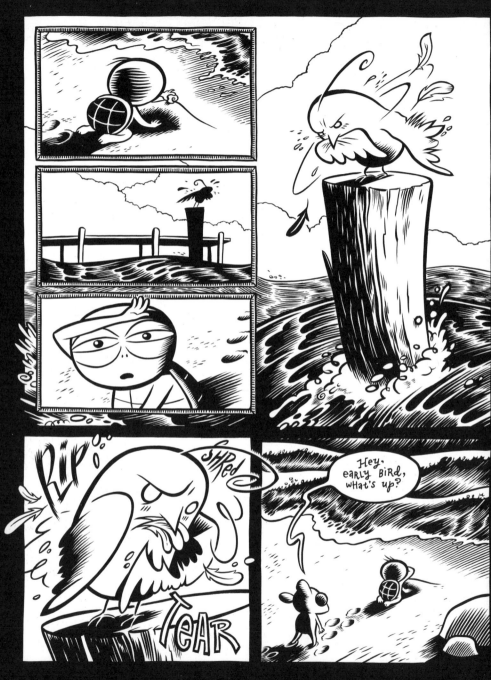

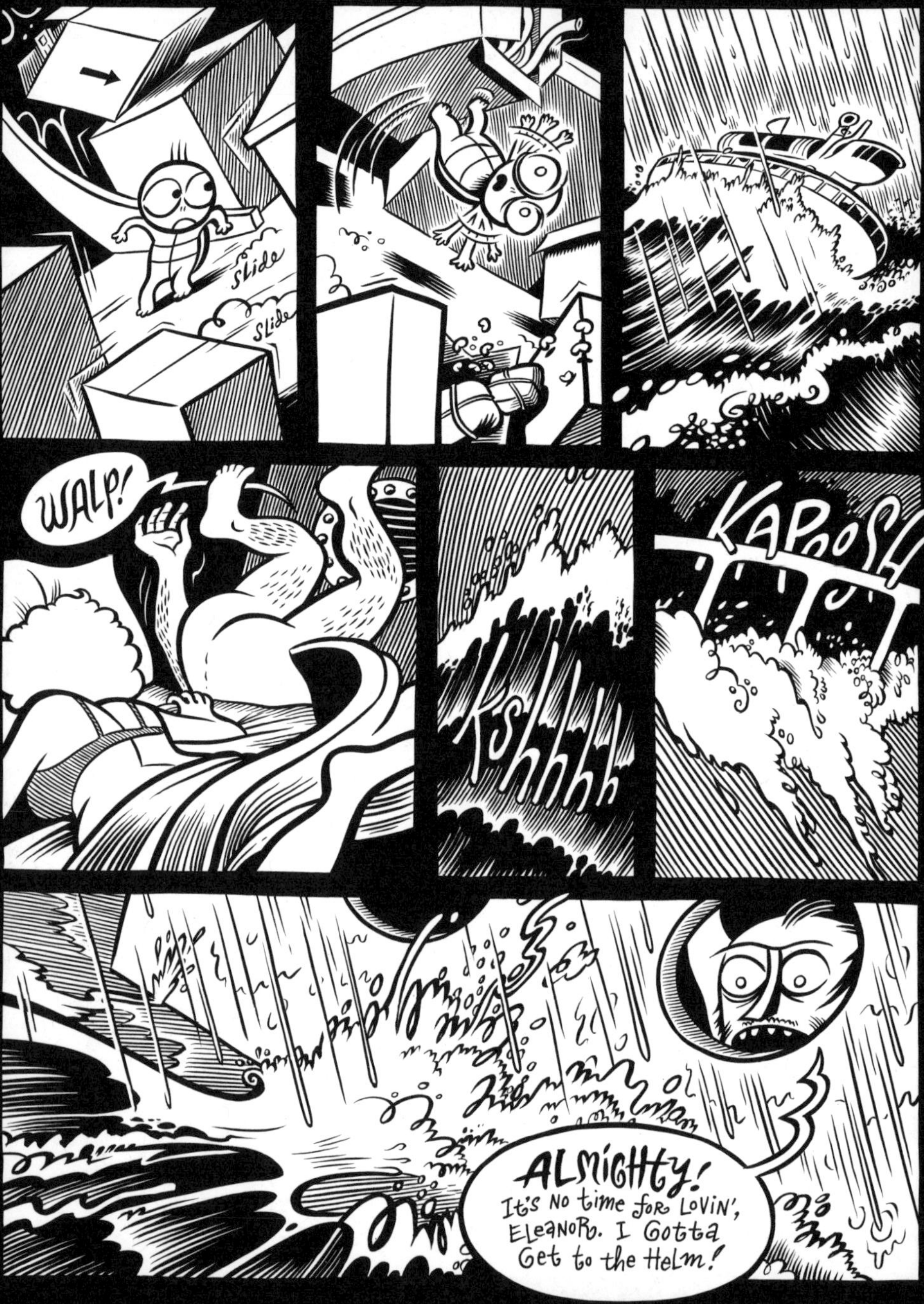
SLide
SLide
WALP!
Kshhhhh
KAPOOSH
ALMIGHTY!
It's No time for LOVIN', ELeanoR. I Gotta Get to the Helm!

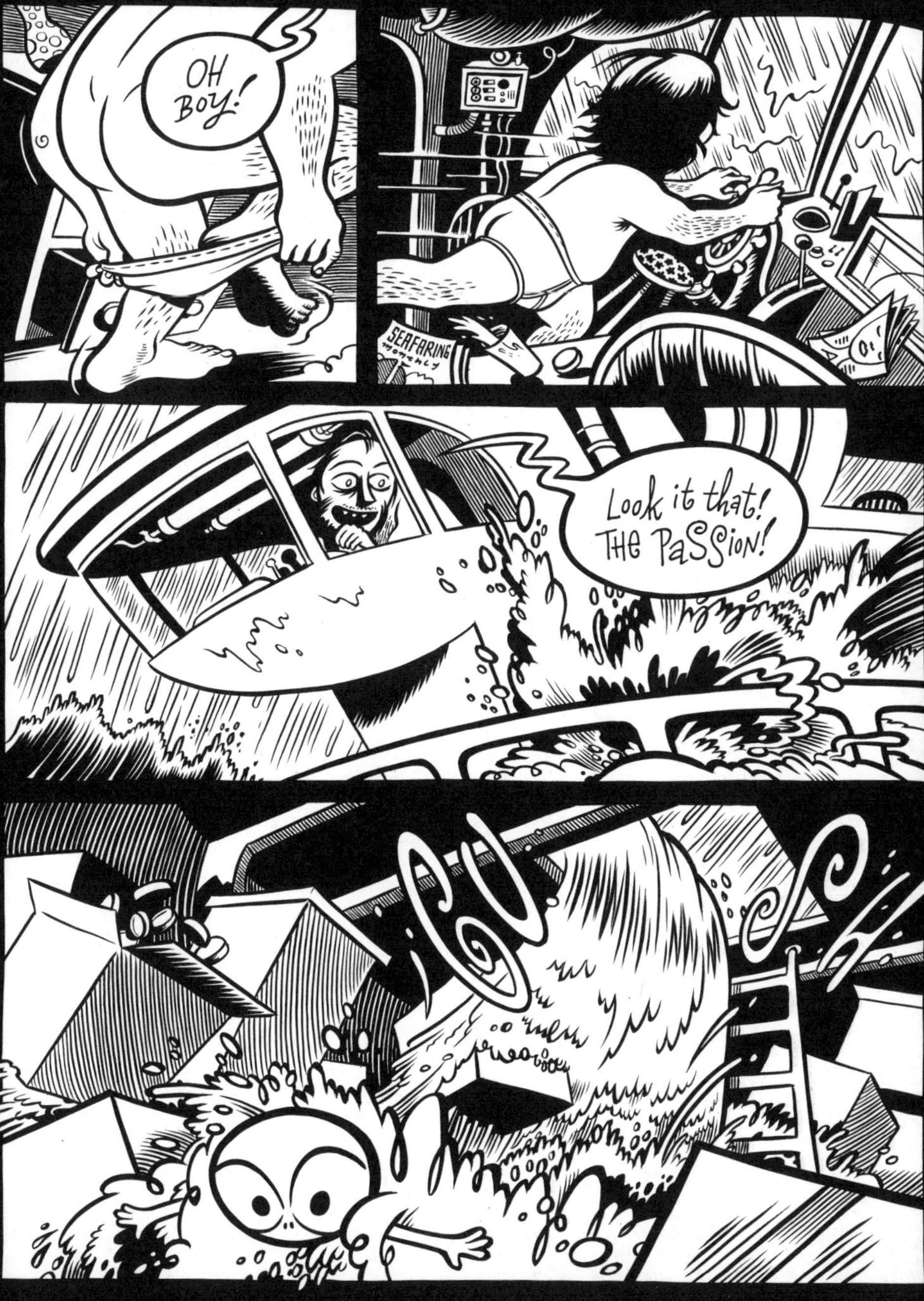
OH Boy!
SEAFARING MONTHLY
Look it that! THE PaSSion!

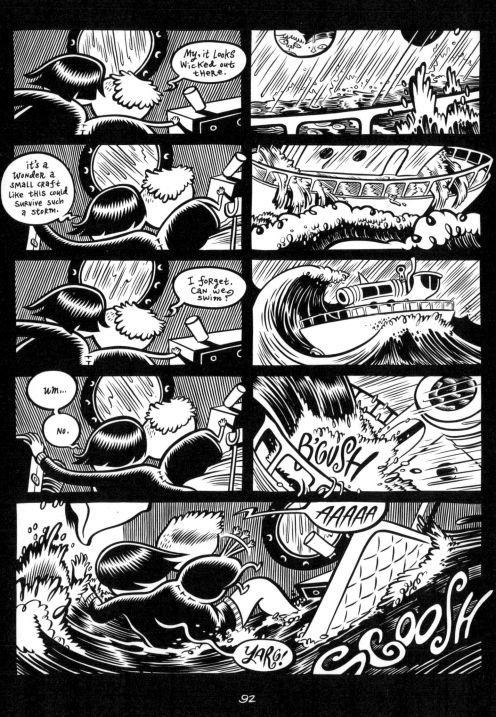

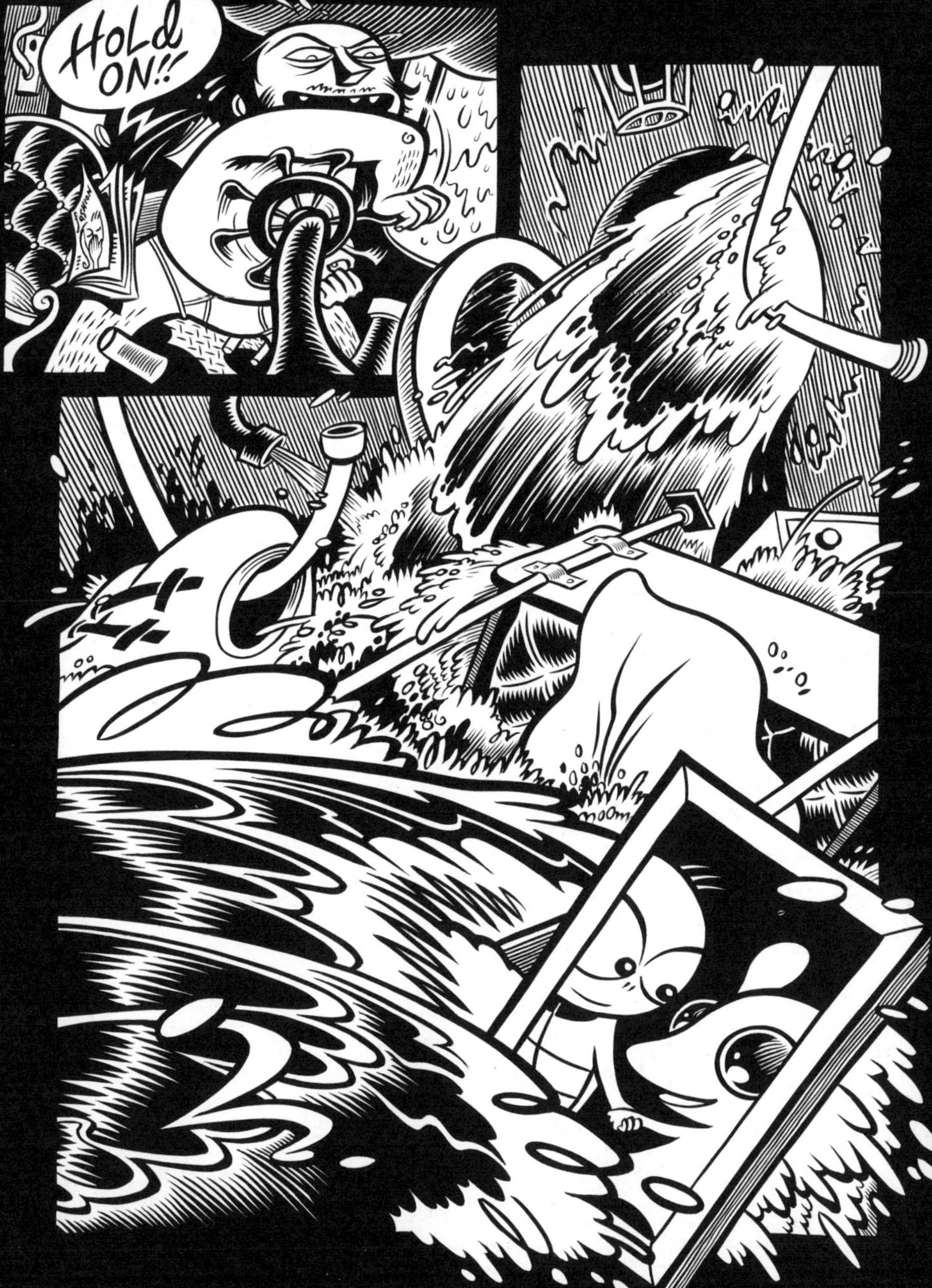
HOLD ON!!

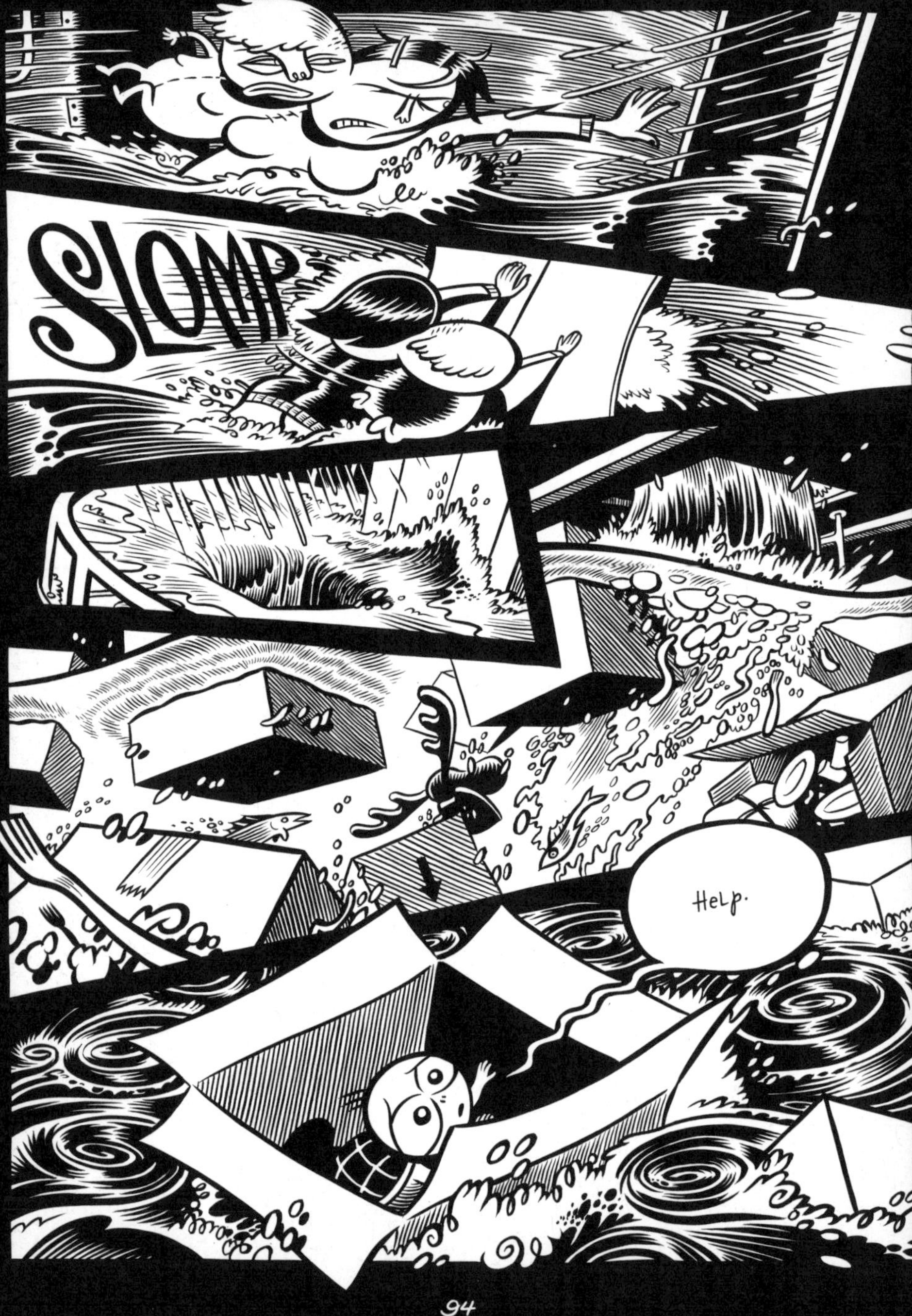
SLOMP
Help.

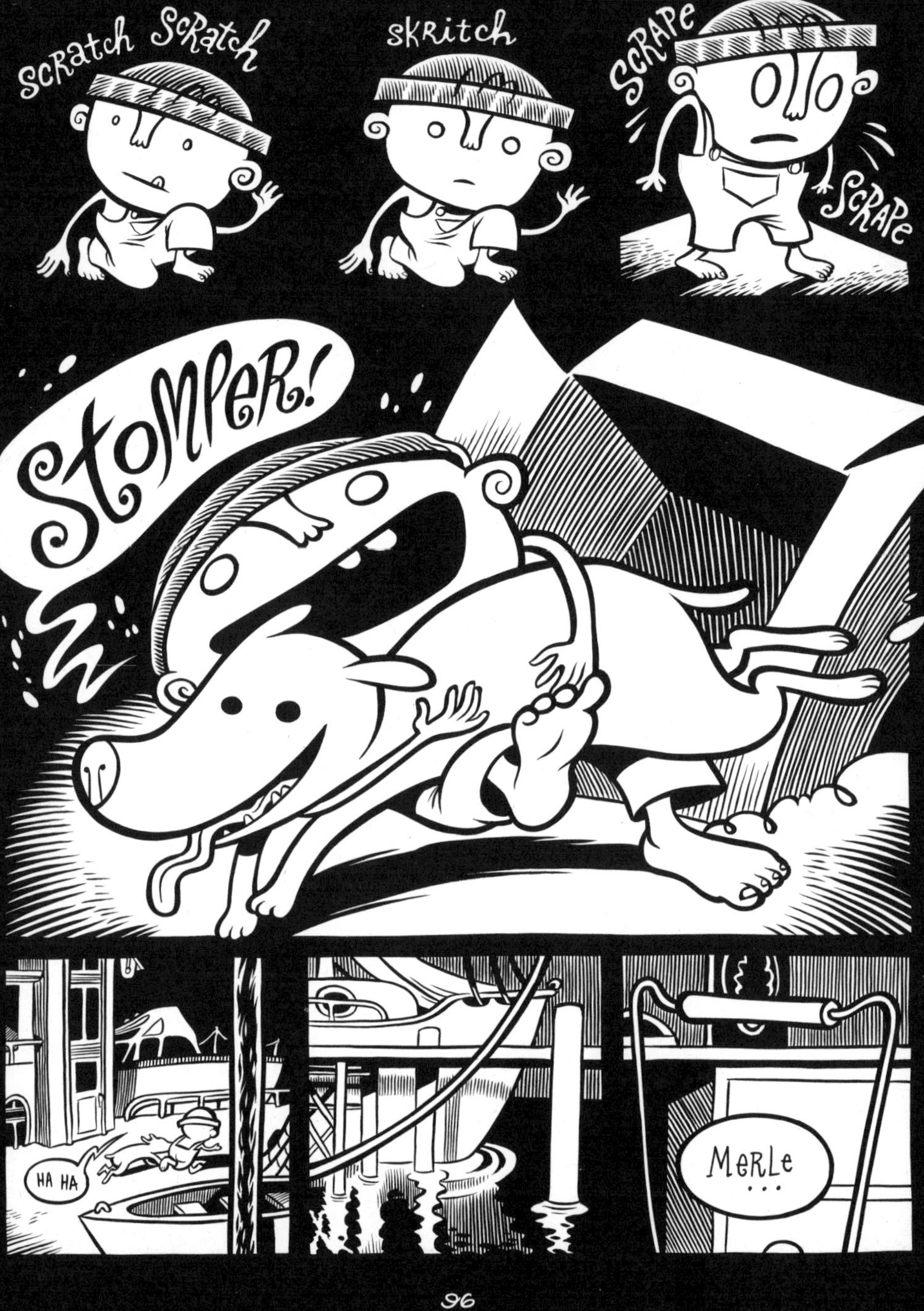
SCRATCH SCRATCH
SKRITCH
SCRAPE
SCRAPE
STOMPER!
HA HA
MERLE
...

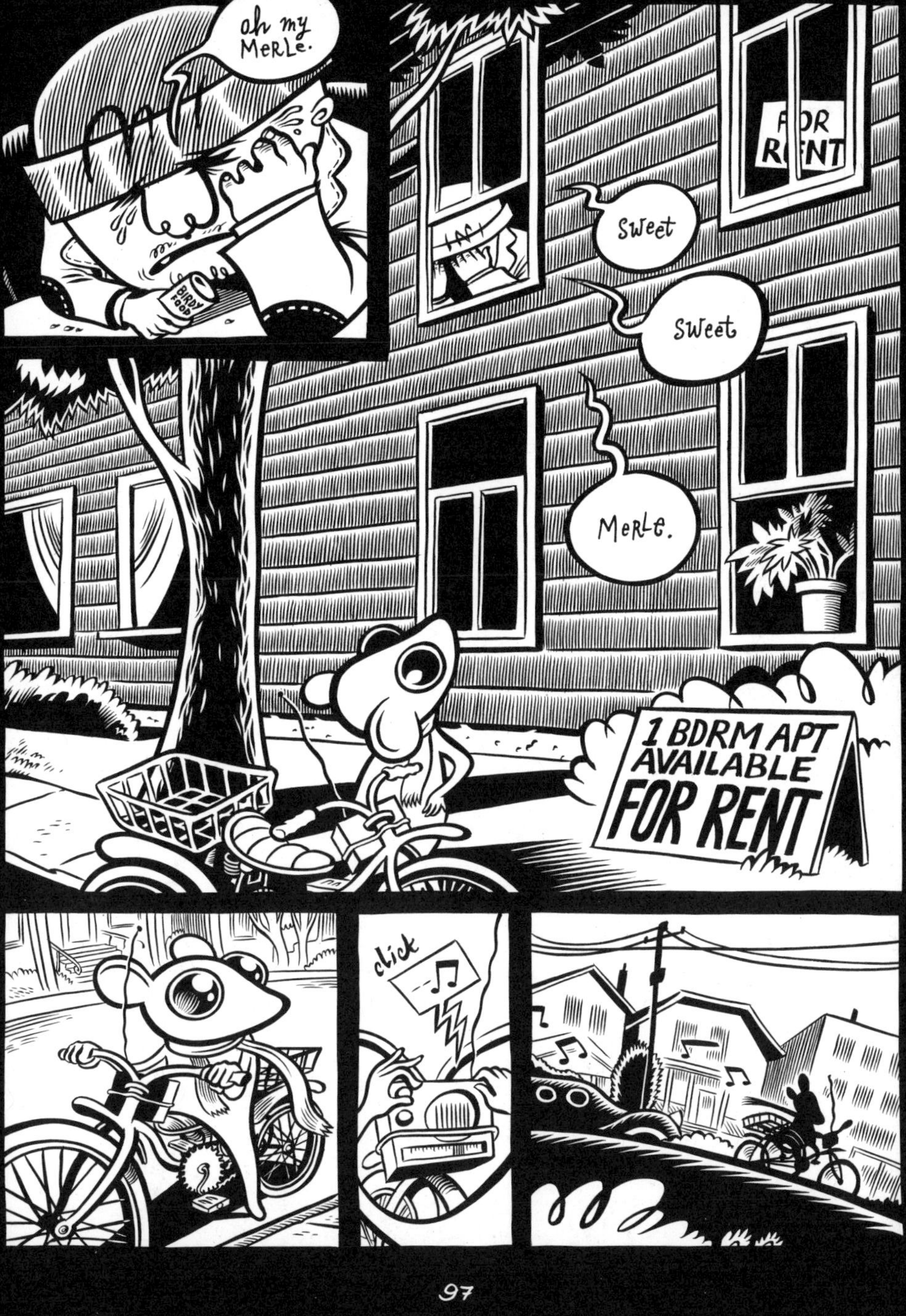
oh my
MERLE.
BIRDY FOOD
FOR
RENT
sweet
sweet
MERLE.
1 BDRM APT
AVAILABLE
FOR RENT
click

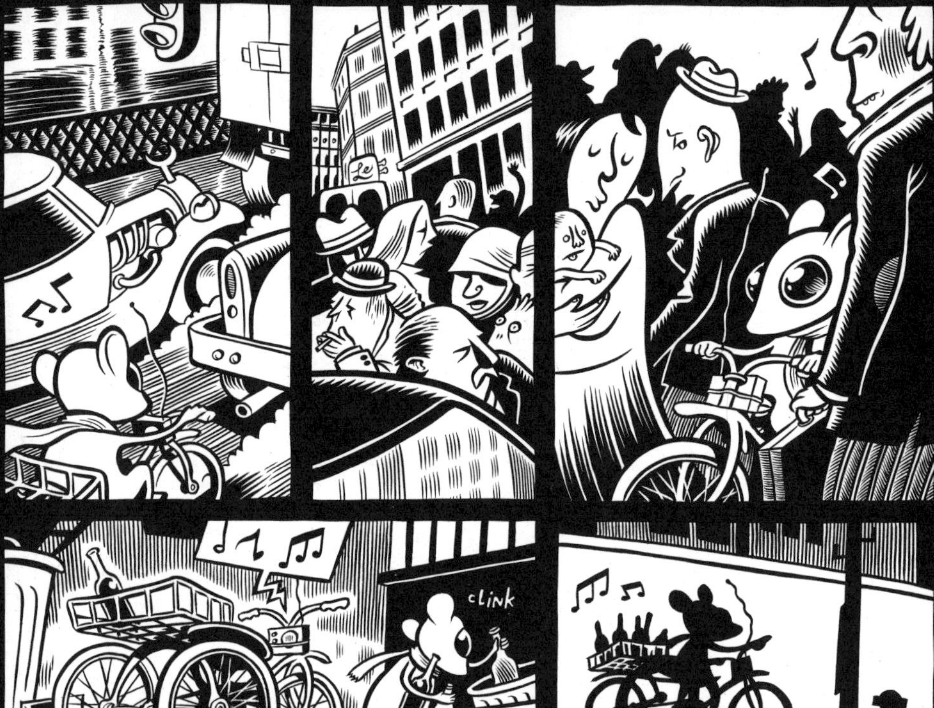
clink

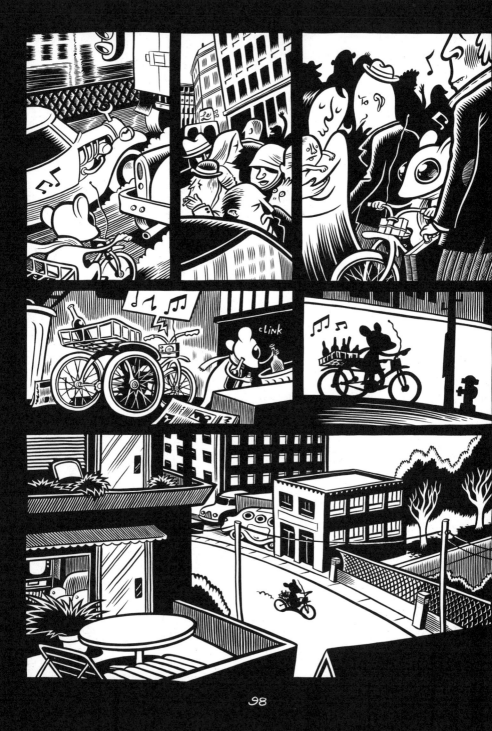

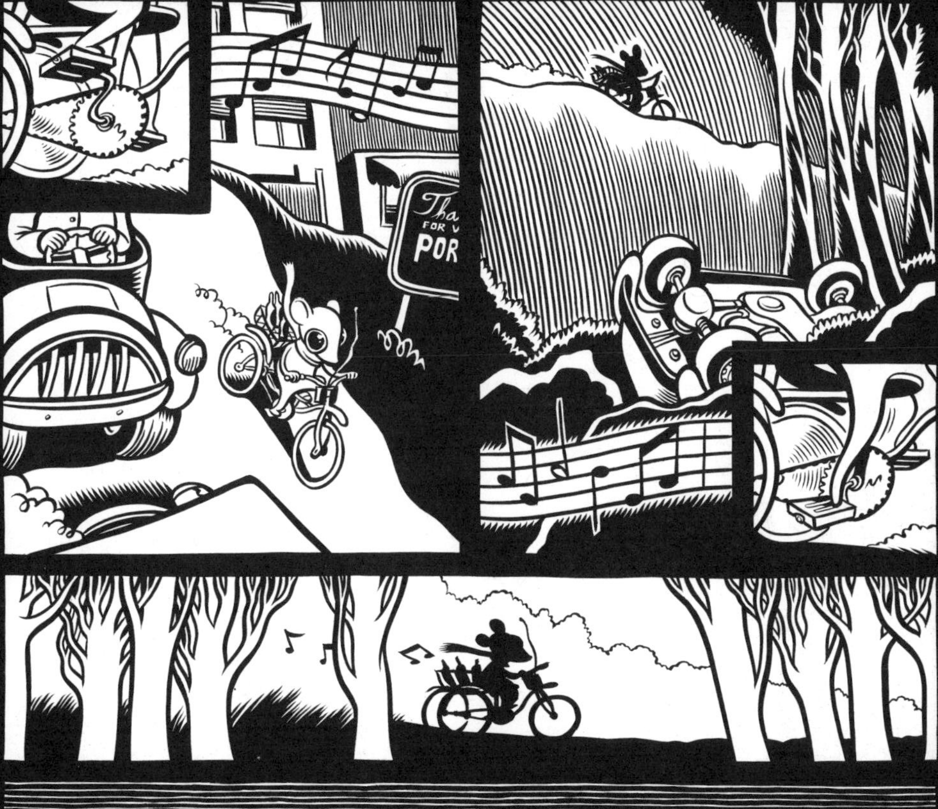
Tha
FOR V
POR

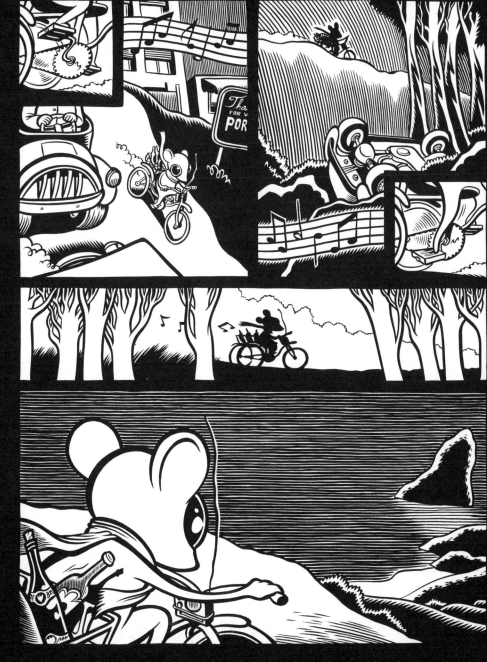

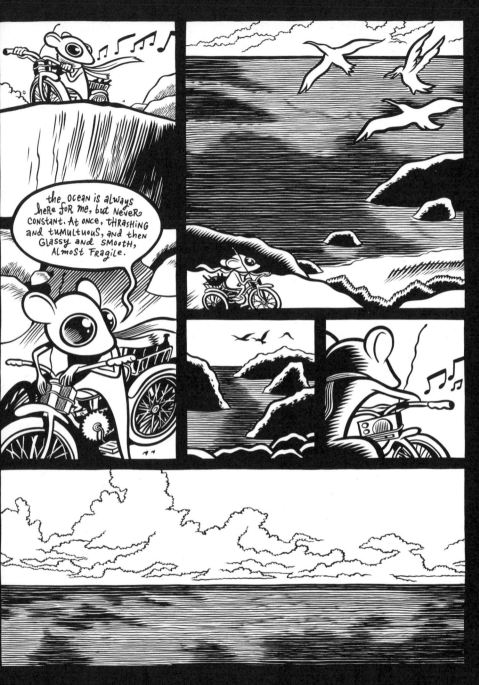

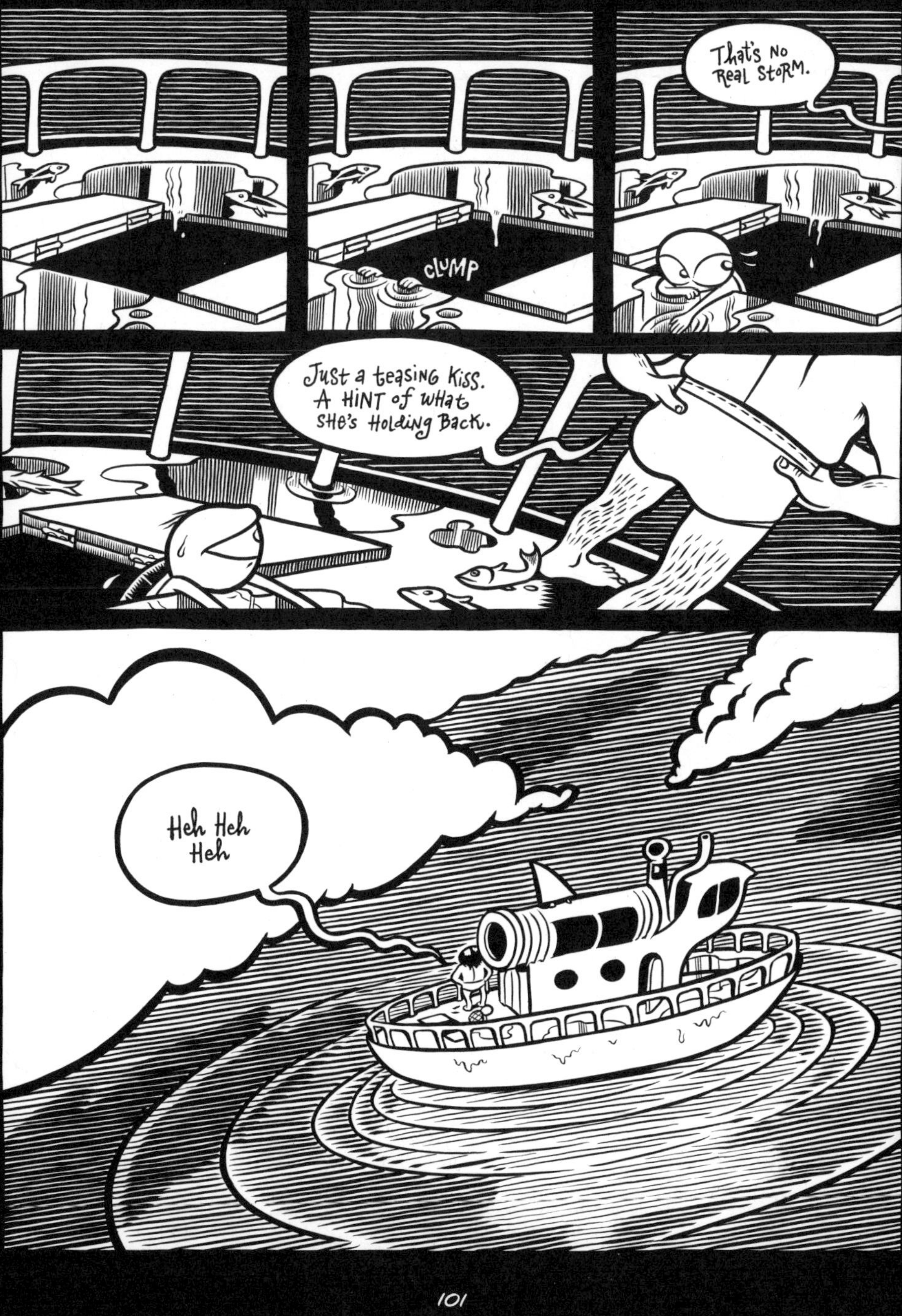
CLUMP
That's no real storm.
Just a teasing kiss. A hint of what she's holding back.
Heh Heh Heh

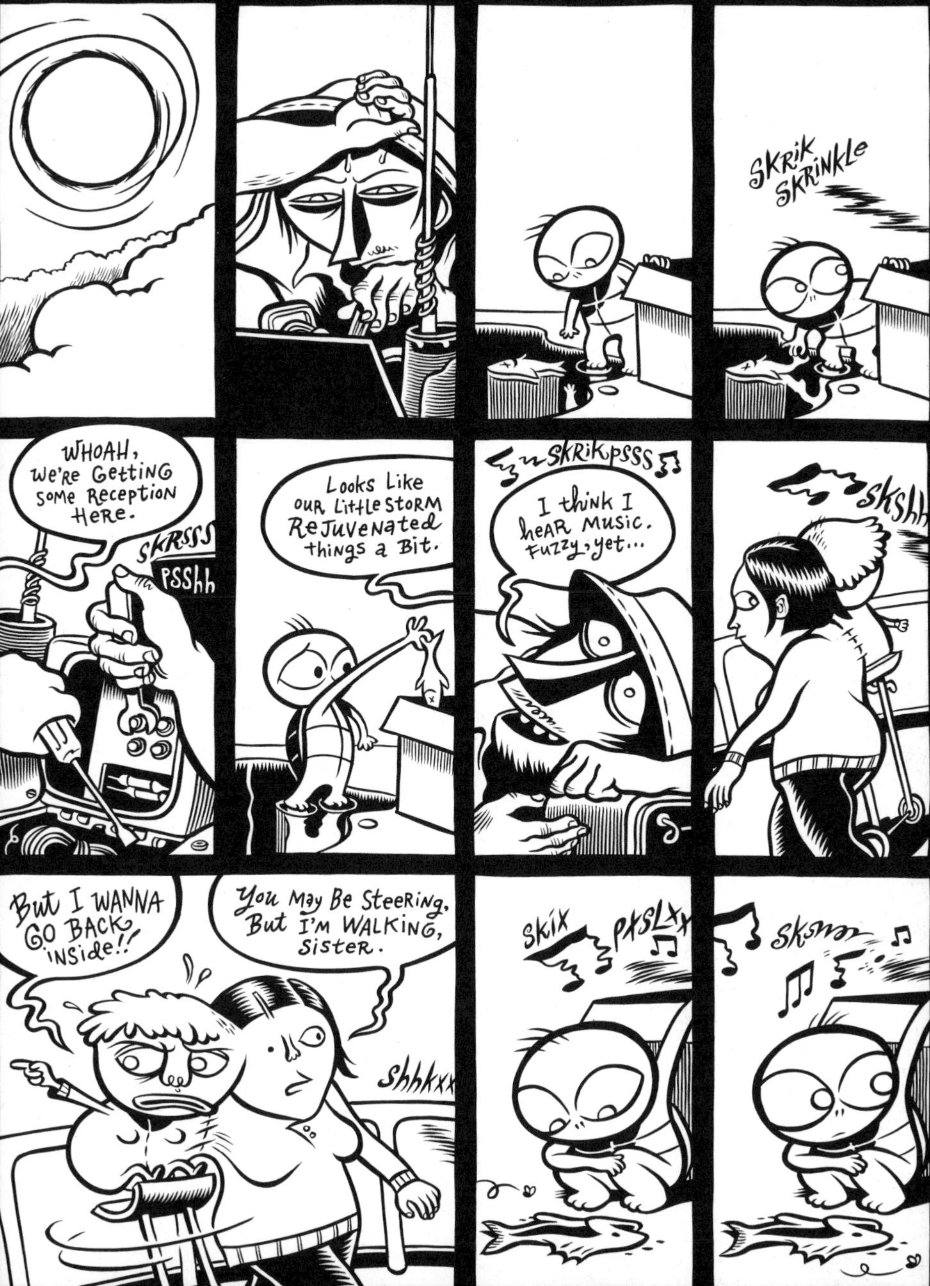
SKRIK
SKRINKLE
WHOAH, WE'RE GETTING SOME RECEPTION HERE.
SKRSSS
PSShh
Looks like our little storm rejuvenated things a bit.
SKRIKPSSS
I think I hear music. Fuzzy, yet...
SKShh
But I WANNA GO BACK inside!!
You may be steering, but I'M WALKING, sister.
Shhkxx
SKIX
PXSLXX
SKSM

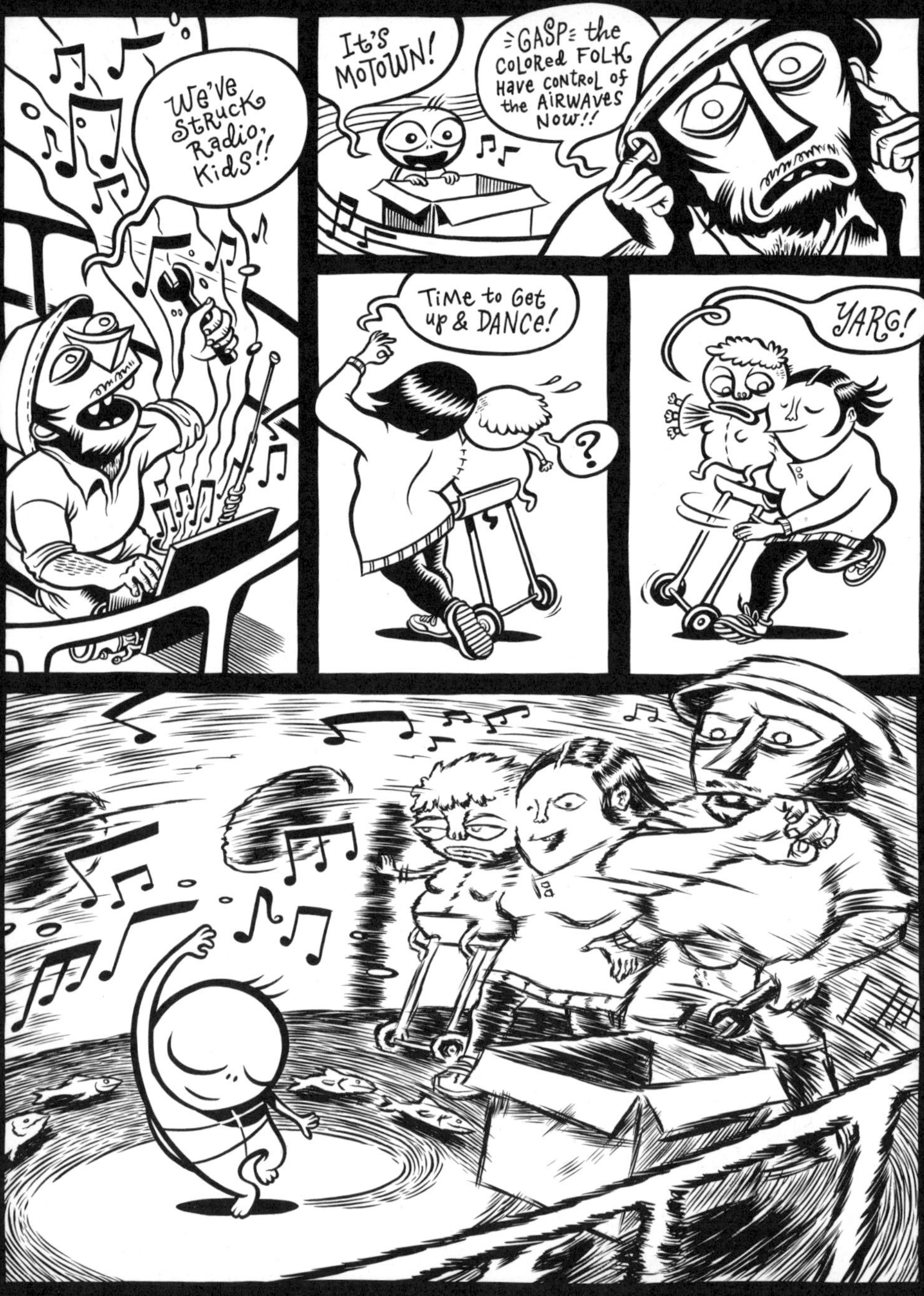
We've Struck Radio, Kids!!
It's MOTOWN!
GASP the Colored FOLK Have CONTROL of the AIRWAVES NOW!!
Time to Get up & DANCE!
?
YARG!

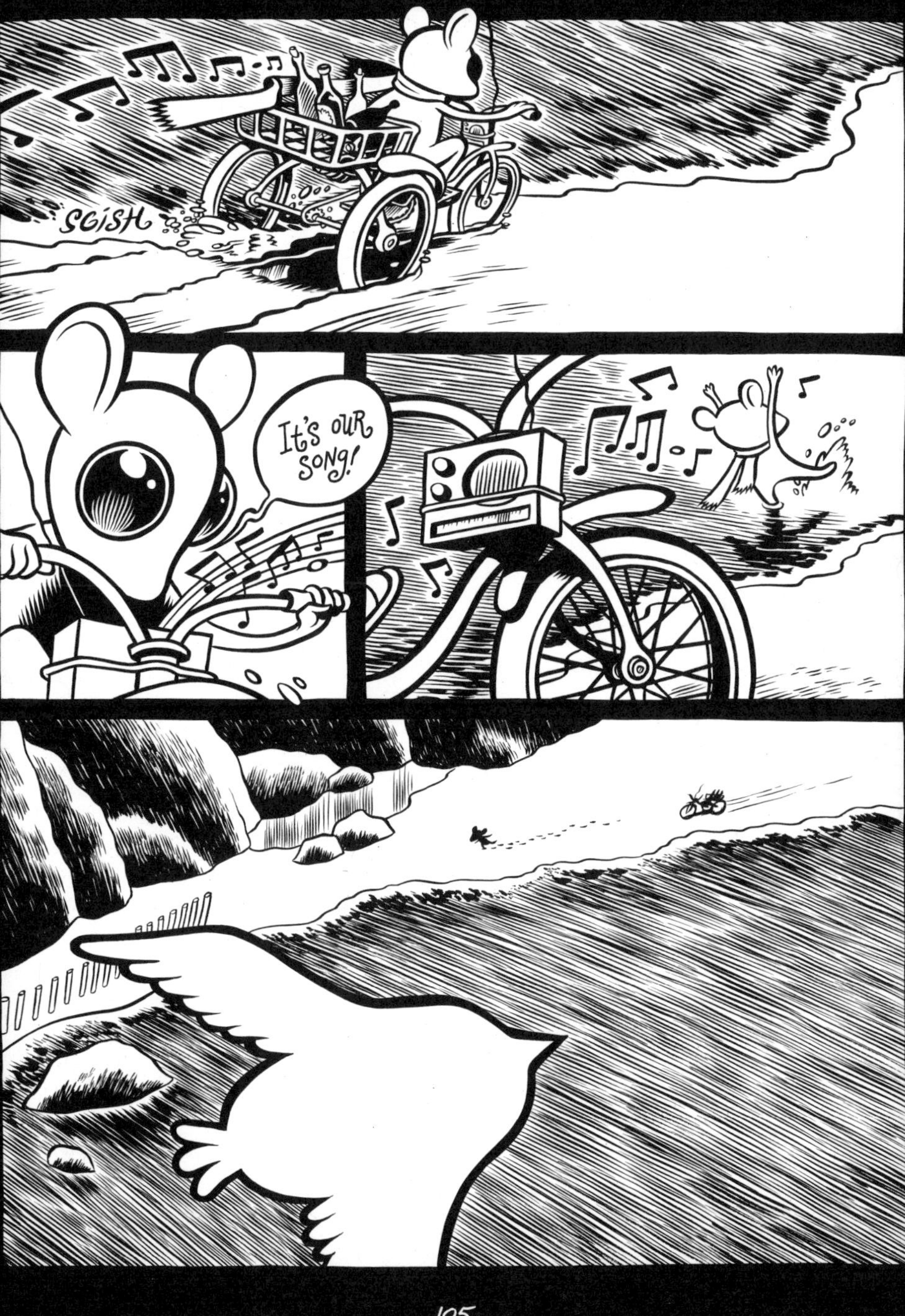
SQISH
It's our song!

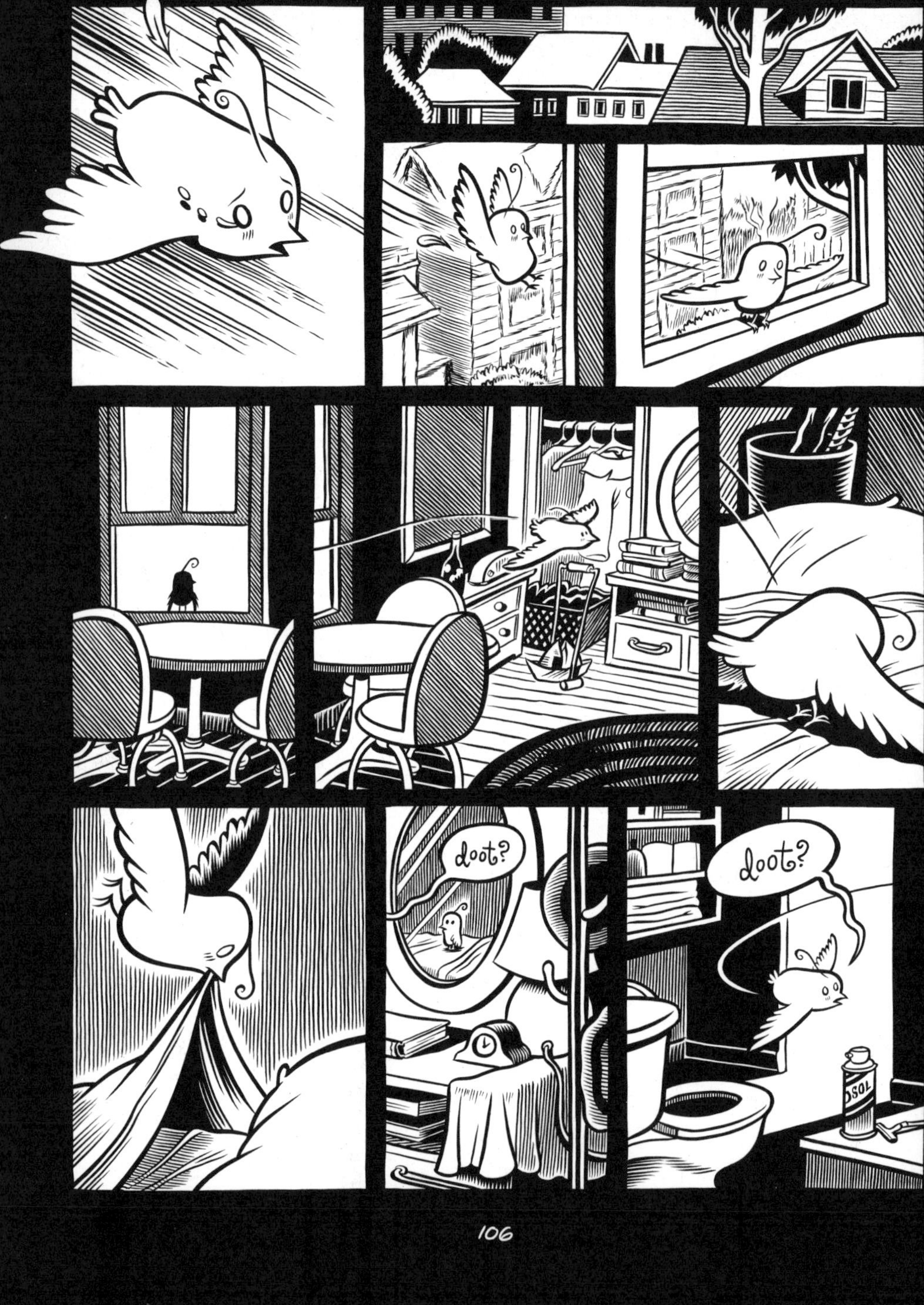
doot?
doot?

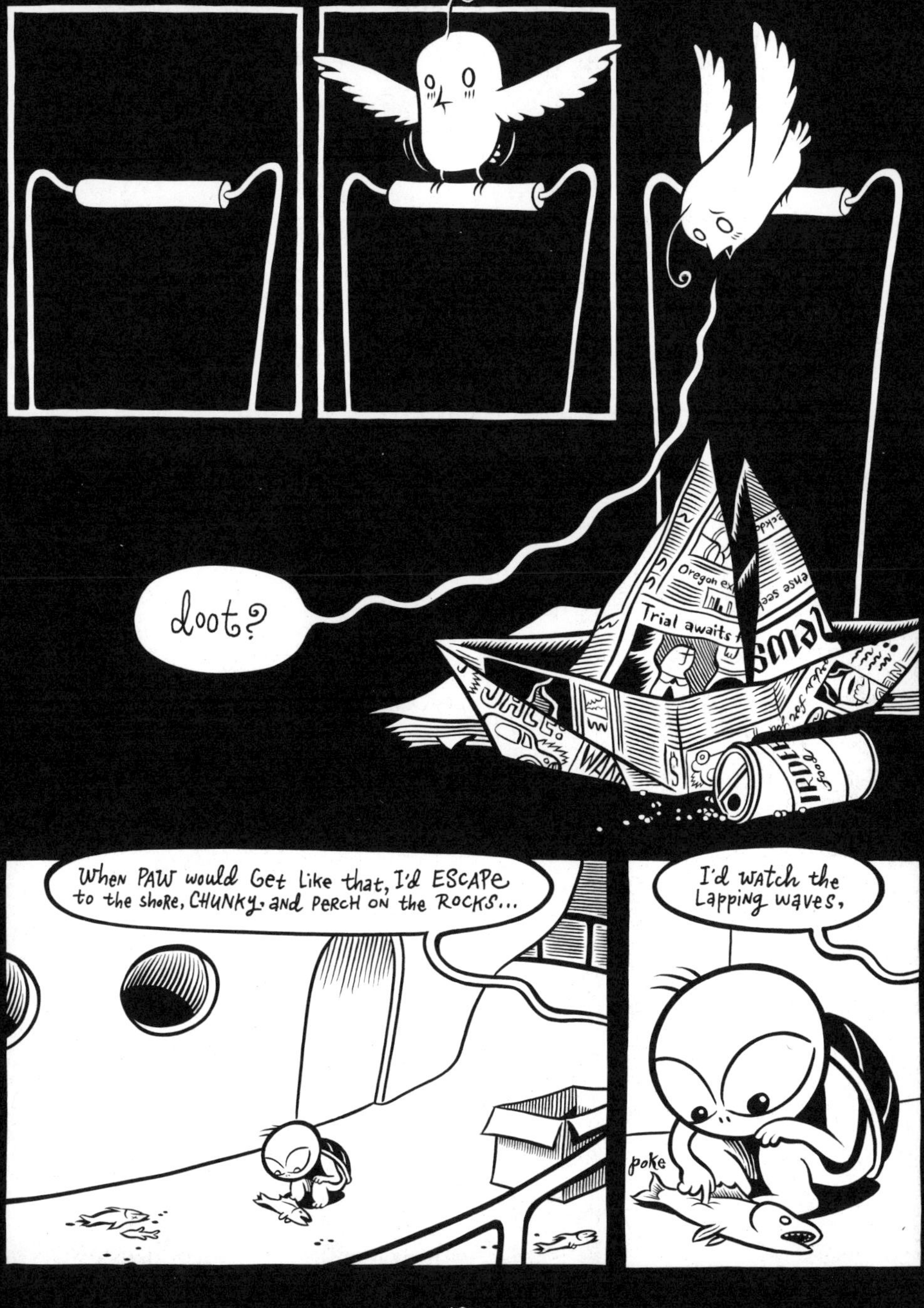
doot?
Oregon ex
Trial awaits
News
When PAW would Get Like that, I'd ESCAPE to the shore, CHUNKY, and PERCH ON the ROCKS...
I'd watch the Lapping waves,
poke

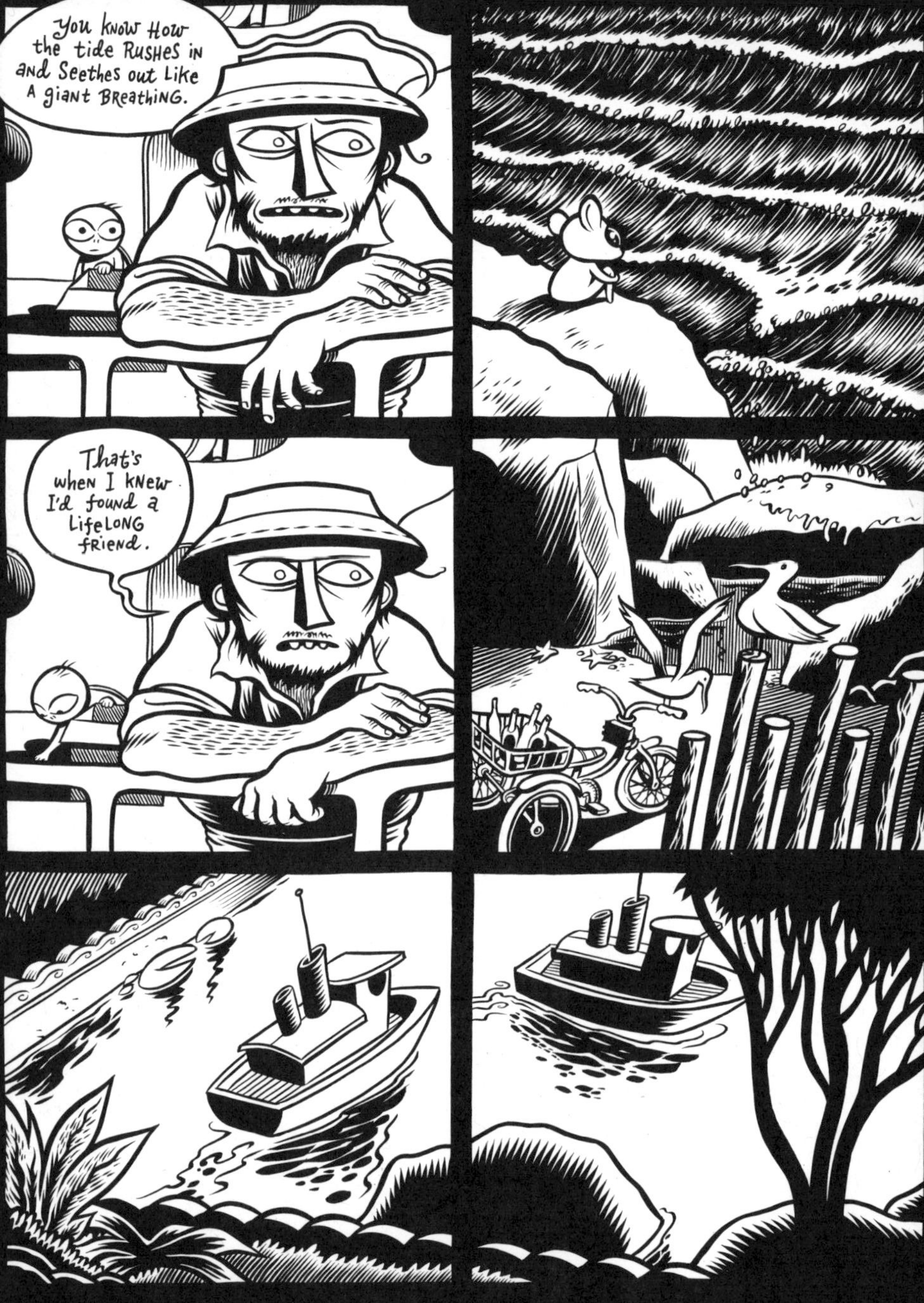
You know How the tide RUSHES IN and Seethes out Like A giant BReathING.
That's when I KNEW I'd found a LifeLONG friend.

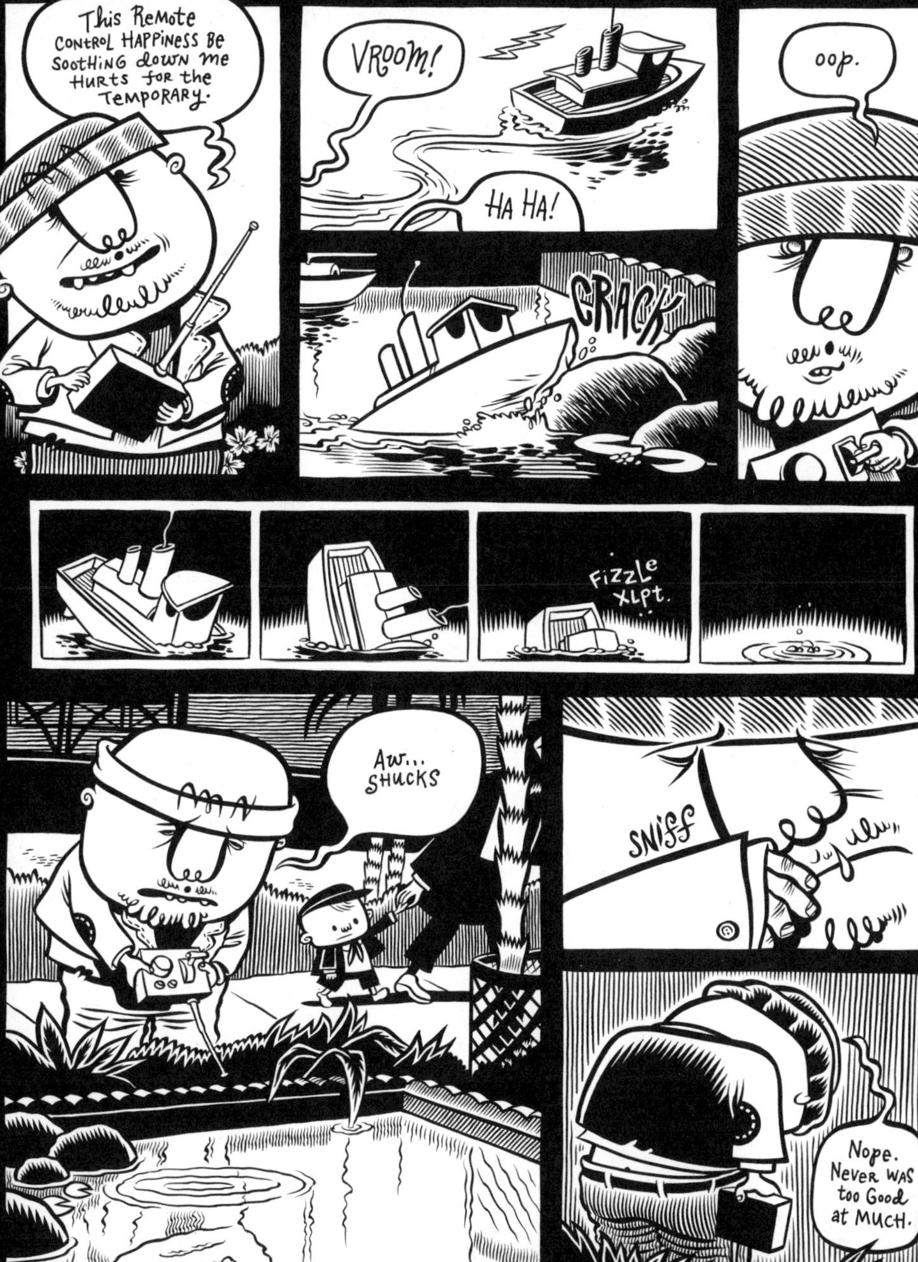
This Remote CONTROL HAPPINESS BE SOOTHING down me HURTS for the TEMPORARY.
VROOM!
HA HA!
CRACK
oop.
FIZZLE
XLPT.
AW... SHUCKS
SNIFF
Nope. NEVER WAS too Good at MUCH.

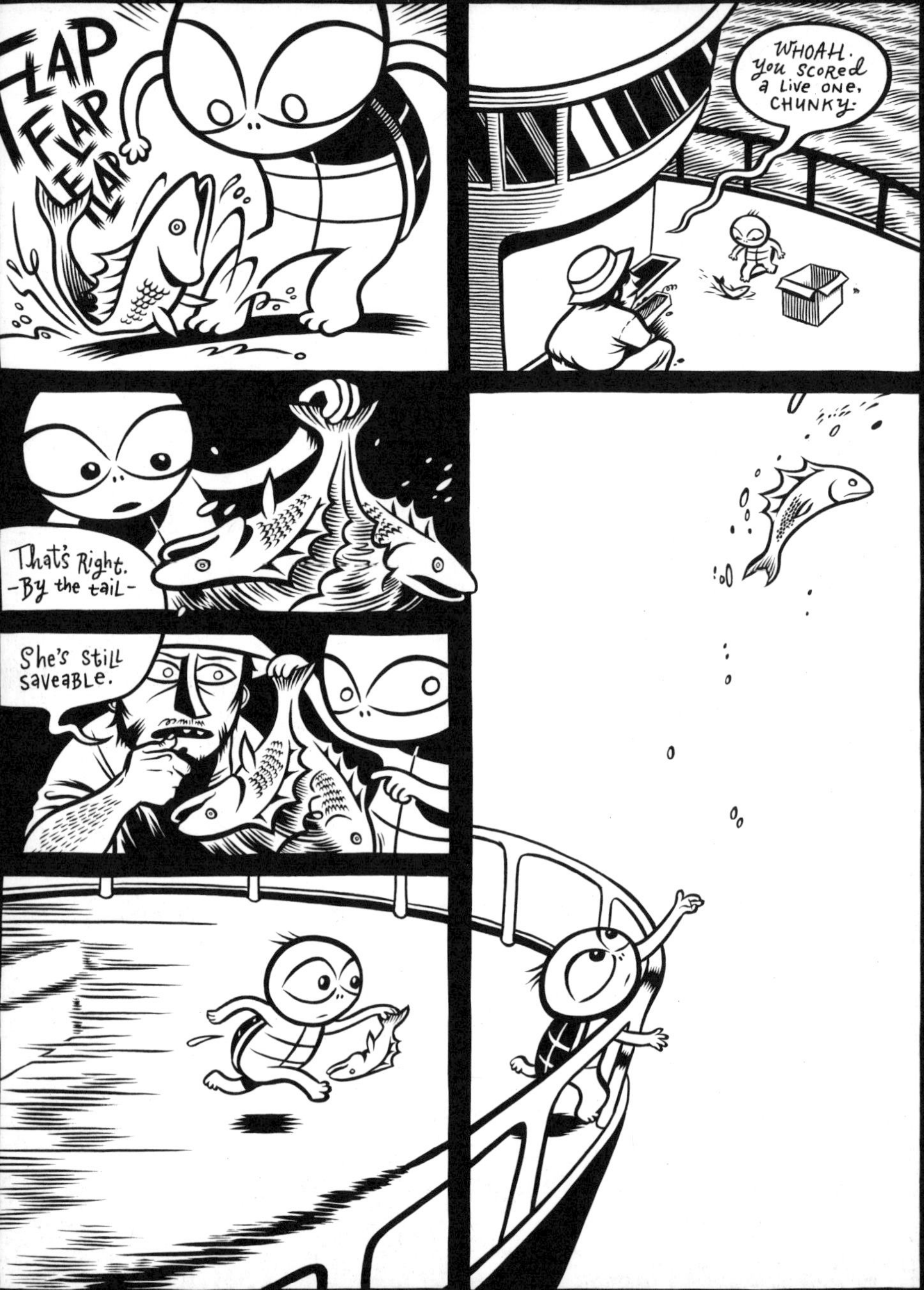
FLAP FLAP FLAP FLAP
WHOAH. You scored a live one, CHUNKY.
That's Right. -By the tail-
She's still saveable.

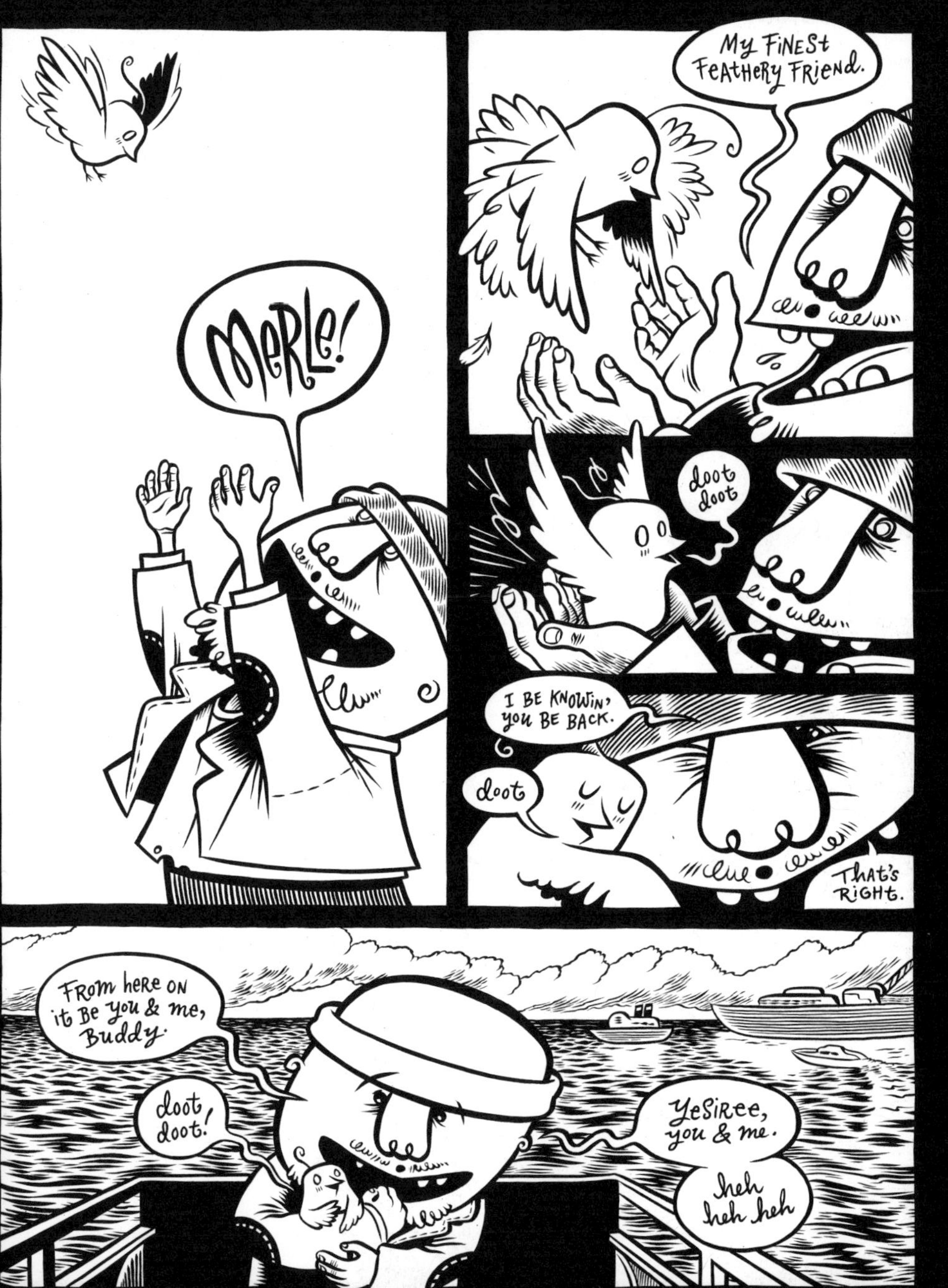
MERLE!
MY FINEST FEATHERY FRIEND.
doot doot
I BE KNOWIN' YOU BE BACK.
doot
THAT'S RIGHT.
FROM here ON it Be you & me, Buddy.
doot, doot!
Yesiree, you & me.
heh heh heh

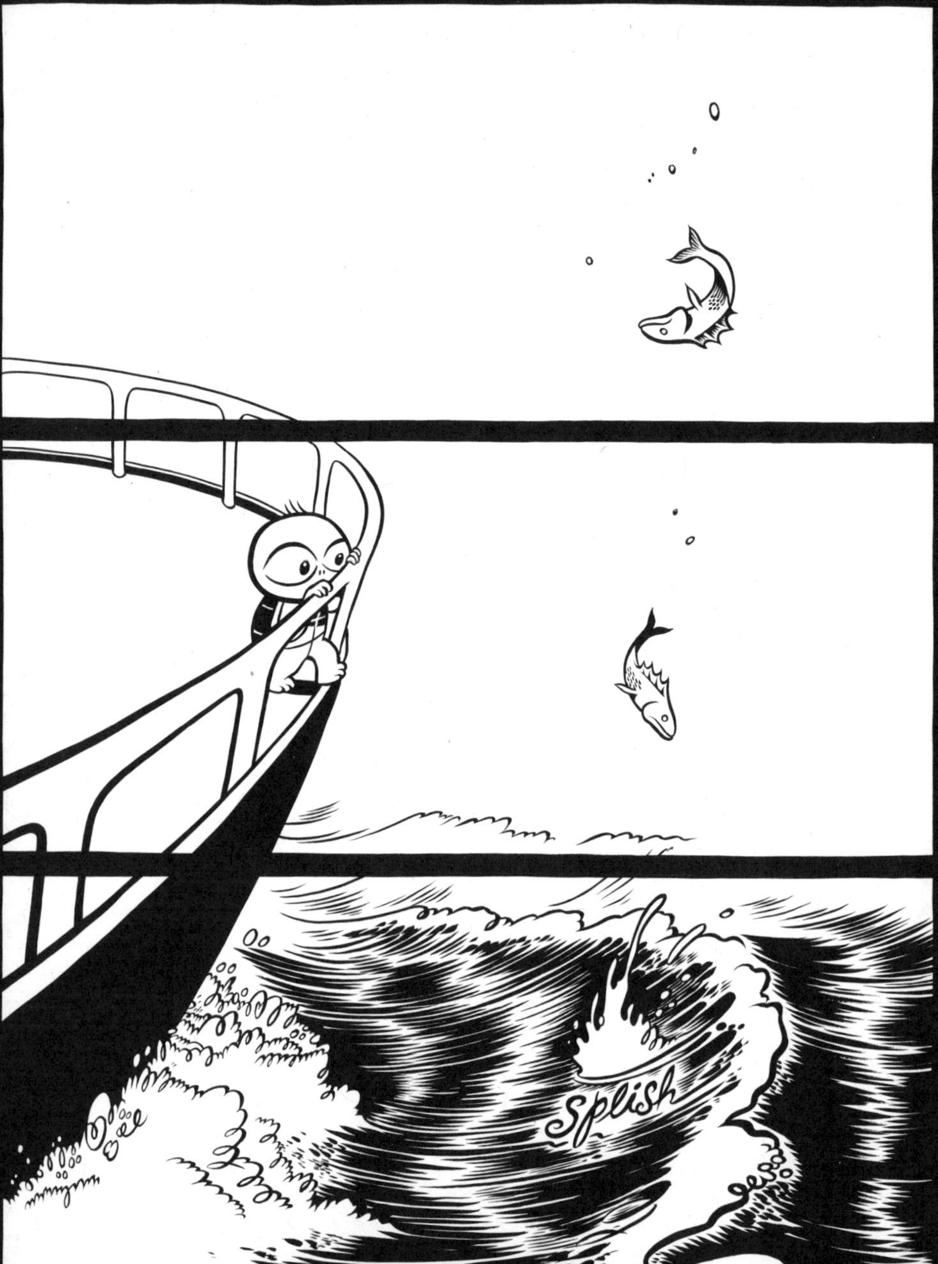
Splish

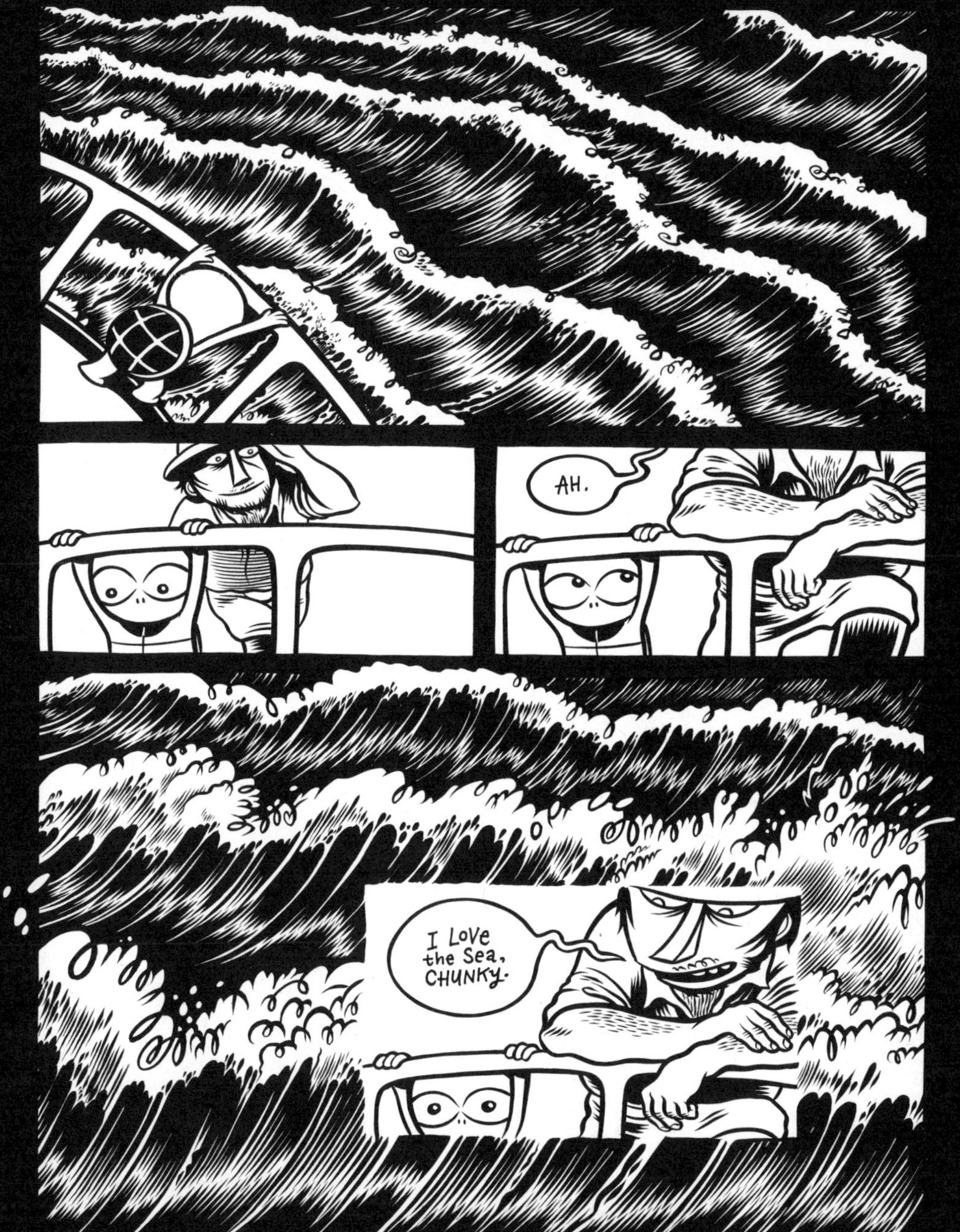
AH.
I Love the Sea, CHUNKY.

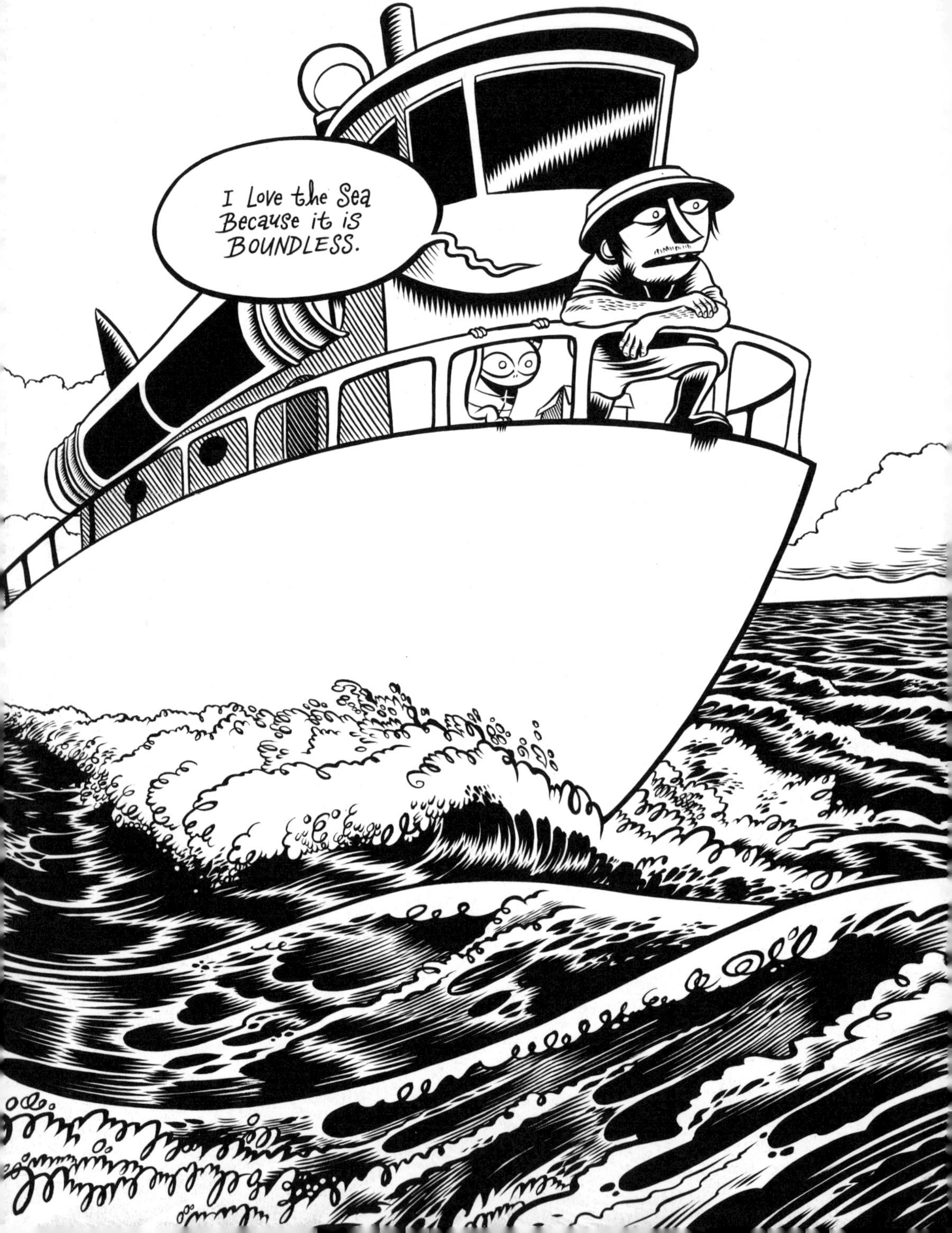
I Love the Sea Because it is BOUNDLESS.

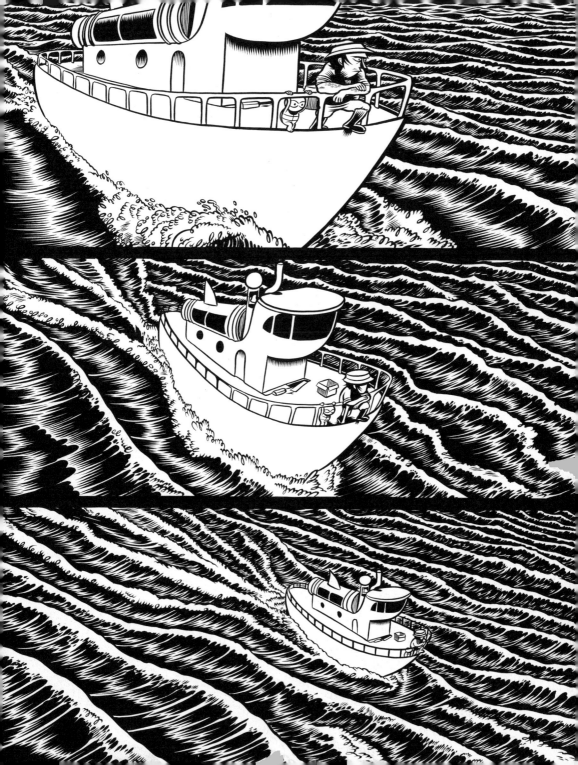

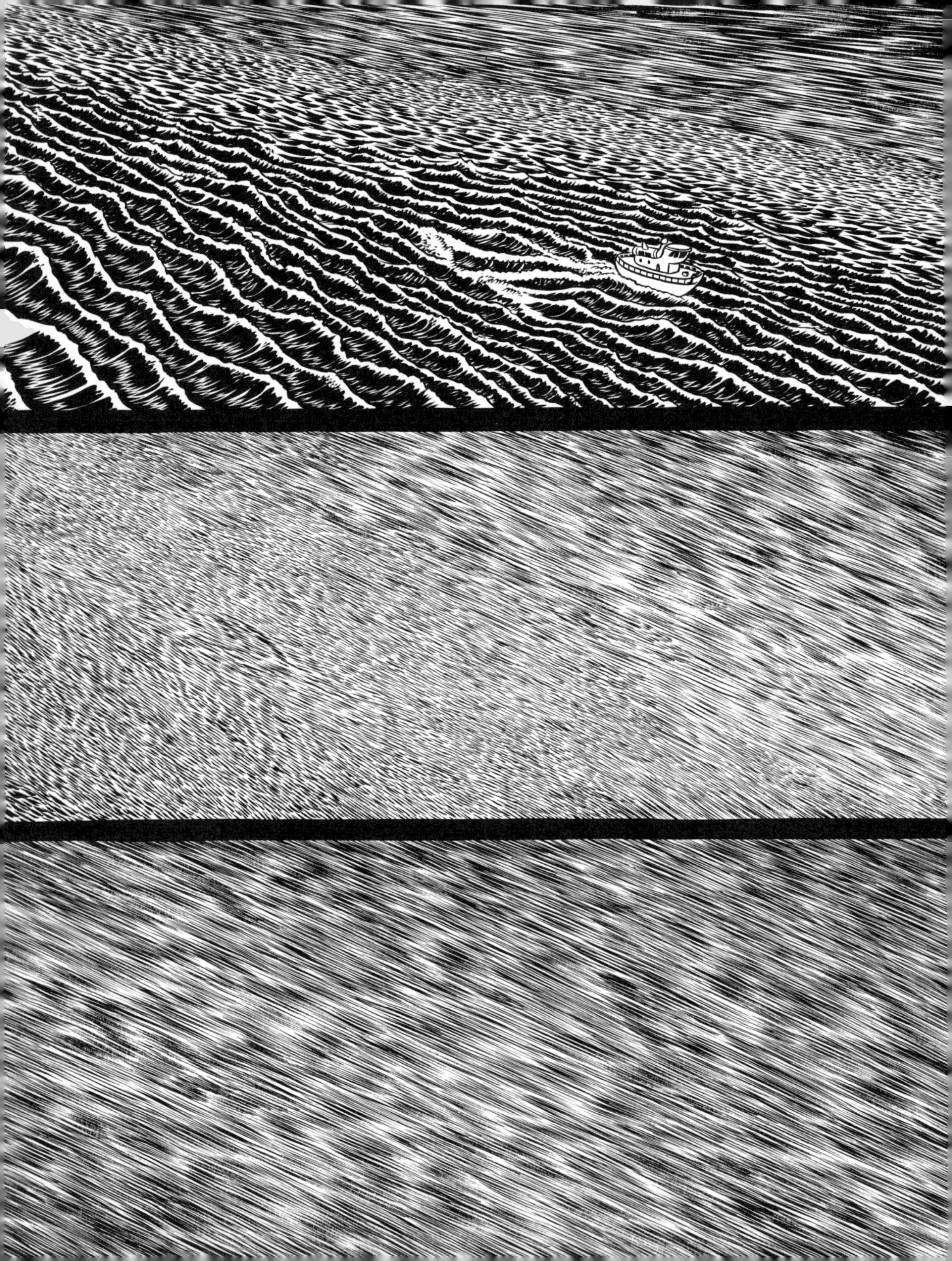

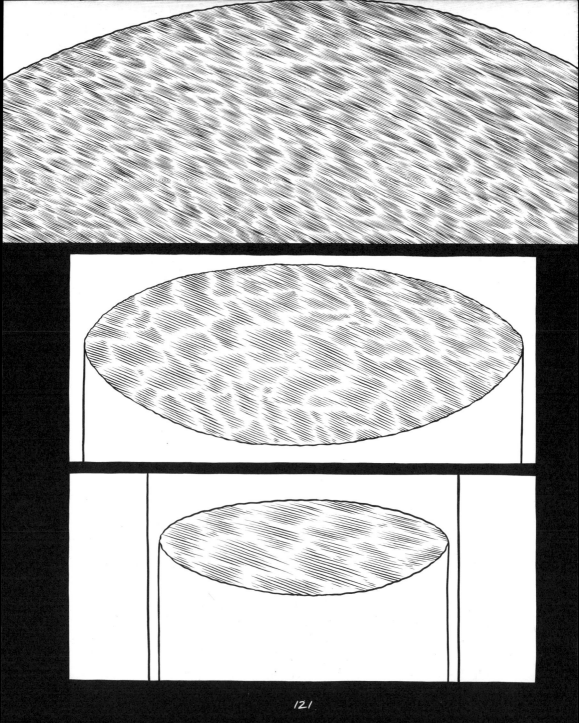

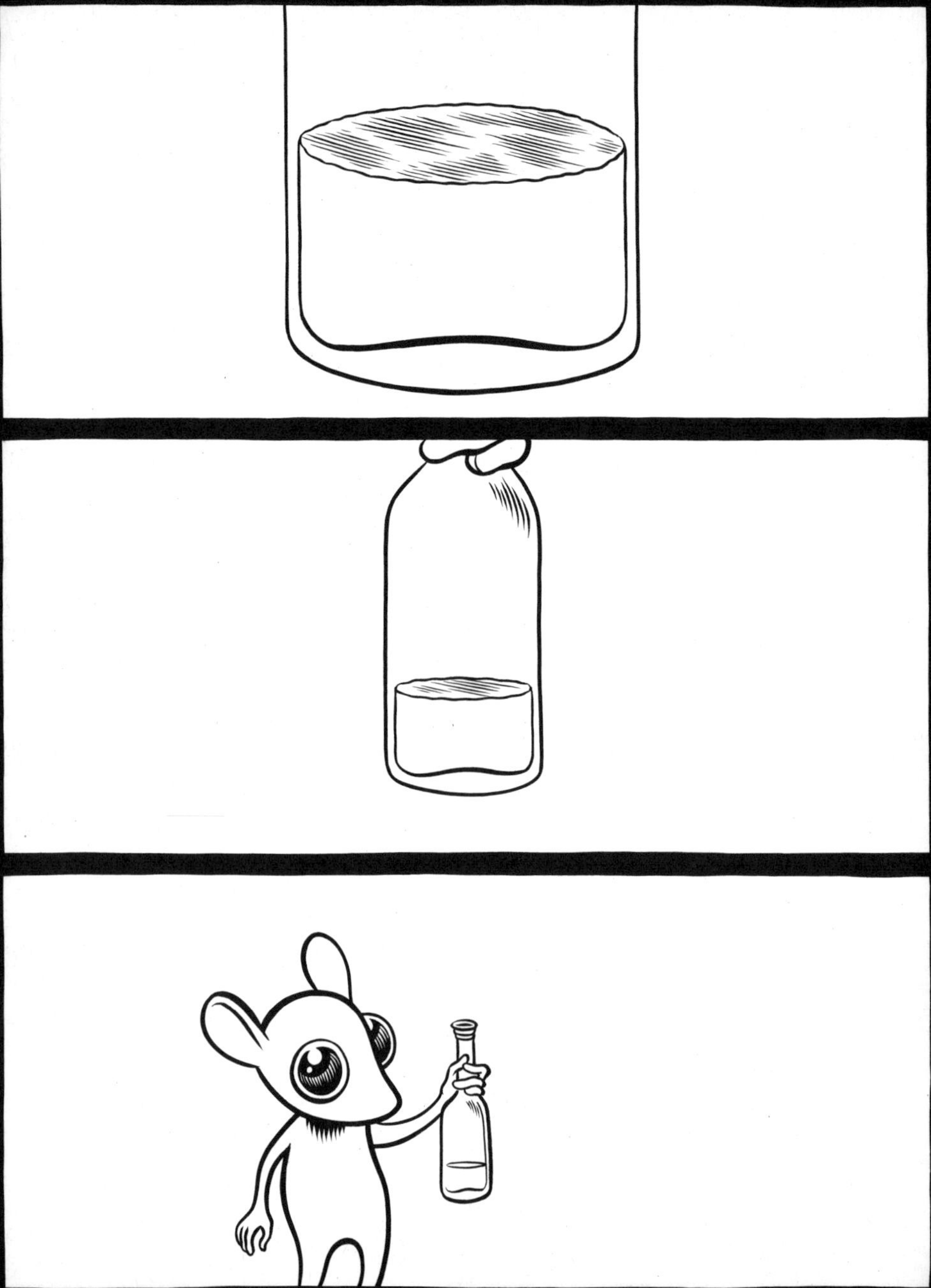

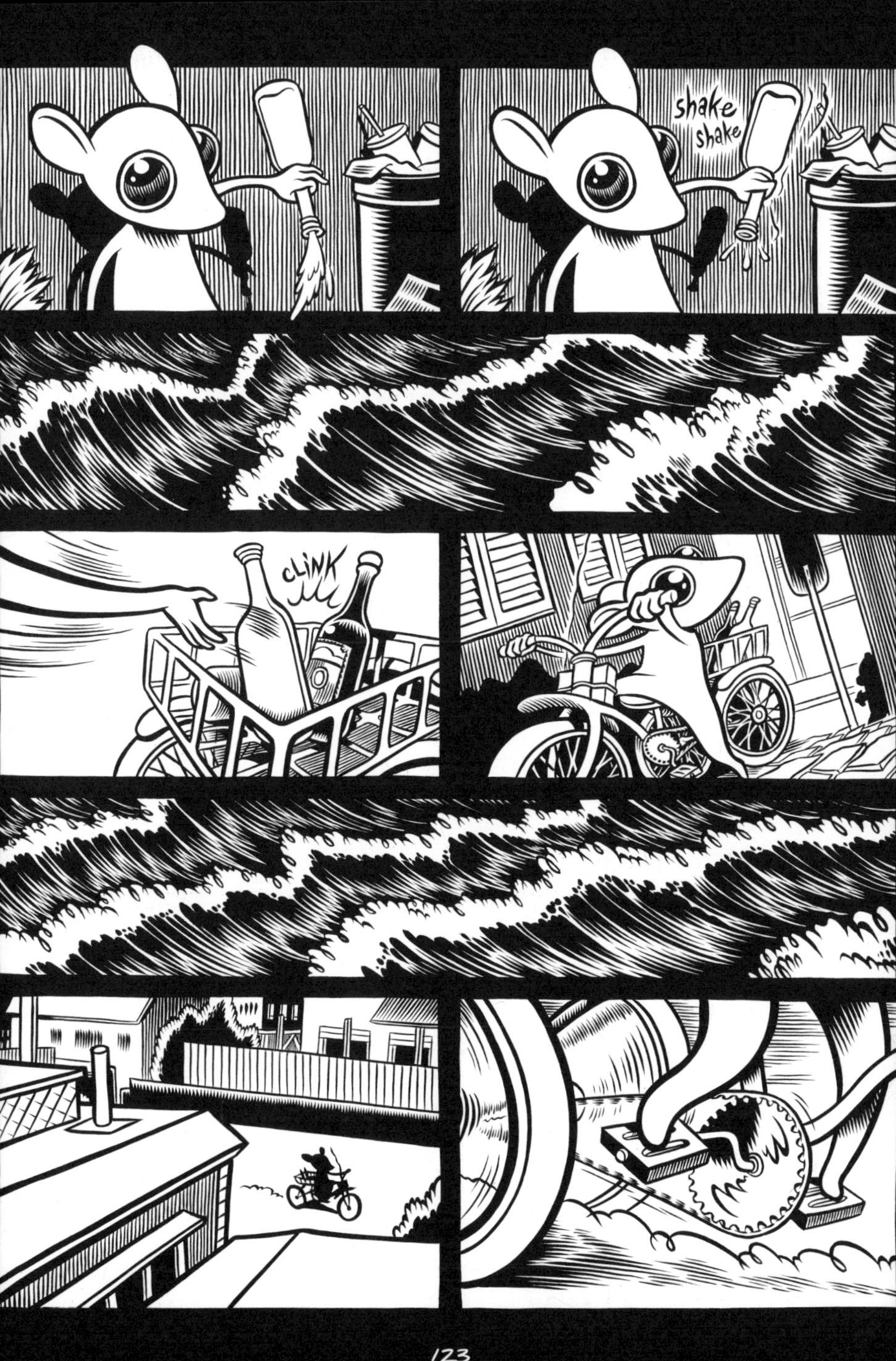
shake
shake
CLINK

There is no Good-bye, Chunky Rice.

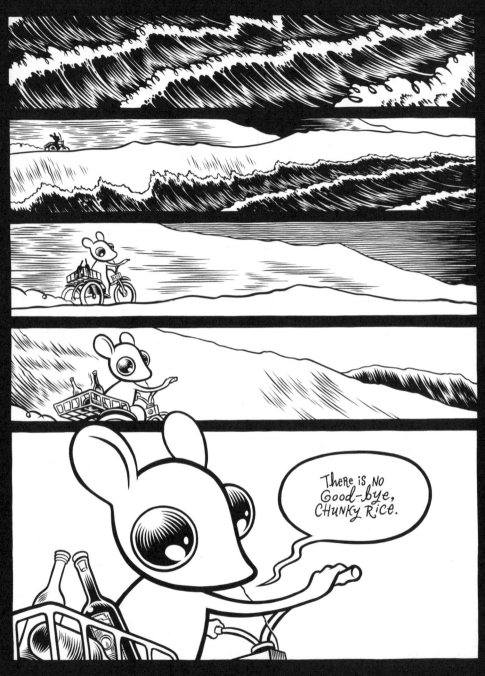

CLUNK